Strategies for Writing
in the
SCIENCE CLASSROOM

Kathleen Kopp

Strategies for Writing in the Science Classroom
By Kathleen Kopp

Cover Design and Layout: Hank McAfee

Library of Congress Cataloging-in-Publication Data
Kopp, Kathleen, 1967-
    Strategies for writing in the science classroom / by Kathleen N. Kopp.
          p. cm.
      Includes bibliographical references.
      ISBN 978-1-937412-01-2 (alk. paper)
    1. Science--Study and teaching. 2. Language arts--Correlation with content subjects.
    3. English language--Composition and exercises--Study and teaching. I. Title.
LB1585.K66 2011
507.1--dc23
               2011029018

Maupin House publishes professional resources for K-12 educators. Contact us for
tailored, in-house training or to schedule an author for a workshop or conference.
Visit www.maupinhouse.com for free lesson plan downloads.

Maupin House Publishing, Inc. by Capstone Professional
1710 Roe Crest Drive
North Mankato, MN 56003
1-800-524-0634
352-373-5546 (fax)
info@maupinhouse.com
www.maupinhouse.com

Printed in the United States of America in Eau Claire, Wisconsin.
082715   009181R

Writing, to me, is thinking on paper. This book is dedicated to all the teachers of the world who are never quite satisfied with the status quo—those who seek to stretch their students' minds as they develop into well-informed, capable problems-solvers of tomorrow.

Table of Contents

WHY WRITE? A CASE FOR RAWAC

Now that the Common Core State Standards (CCSS) have refocused attention on reading and writing in all subject areas, science teachers are now writing teachers, too.

> "The Standards insist that instruction in reading, writing, speaking, listening, and language be shared responsibly within the school. The K-5 standards include expectations for reading, writing, speaking, and listening and language applicable to a range of subjects, including but not limited to ELA. The grades 6-12 standards are divided into two sections, one for ELA and the other for history/social studies, science, and technical subjects. This division reflects the unique, time-honored place of ELA teachers in developing students' literacy skills while at the same time recognizing that teachers in other areas must have a role in this development as well."

> -Introduction, Common Core State Standards for English Language Arts
> & Literacy in History/Social Studies, Science, and Technical Subjects

For the past decade, research has consistently emphasized the need for accomplished writers in the work force. The National Commission on Writing (2003) contends that the "quality of writing [in classrooms] must improve if students are to succeed in college and in life" (p. 7). In a survey of 120 major American corporations, the Commission (2004) discovered that "writing is a ticket to professional opportunity" (p. 3). The business community identified writing as a "threshold skill" for employees, and it voiced dissatisfactions with the writing competency of college-bound students.

In his research, education expert Tony Wagner (2008) found that business leaders complain more about young employees' "fuzzy thinking" and "lack of writing with a real *voice*" than about poor grammar, punctuation, or spelling. Yet, English classes often address the latter more often than the former. It's not that students cannot write, but that they cannot write well.

The National Assessment of Educational Progress (NAEP) concludes that few students can produce precise, engaging, and coherent papers. According to 1998 National Writing Achievement scores, although a majority of students (78-84 percent of fourth, eighth, and twelfth graders) have at or above basic writing skills, no more than 27 percent of them are at or above proficient. Only 1 percent is advanced.

The National Commission on Writing in America's Schools and Colleges (2003) proclaims that a writing revolution will "put language and communication in their proper place in the classroom"

(p. 3). They recommend creating a writing agenda for the nation. This includes, but is not limited to the following.

1. doubling the amount of time students spend writing

2. writing across the curriculum

3. assigning out-of-school time for written assignments

The bottom line: Employers expect their employees to provide written and oral reports that are accurate, clear, focused, grammatically correct, and appropriate to format and audience. Our students will be spending time writing informational writing, such as technical summaries and research reports connected to their line of work. Their future projects directly relate to how well they can interpret and communicate knowledge they are learning right now in their subject-area classes. Law students reflect on history and government. Aerospace engineers use math and science. Software designers use technical language.

Since the writing our students will engage in as adults is related to specific content, they need practice learning how to write within their current subject areas. This skill will serve them well later.

The strategies in this resource show teachers how to use writing as a way to learn a subject area, as well as a way to demonstrate that learning. Writing, embedded within science classrooms throughout the learning process, will provide students with the practice they need to perform well in their jobs later. The strategies in this book provide content area teachers with several ready-to-go, easy-to-implement strategies that can be used as part of any everyday instruction in their science classrooms.

Writing is a skill best acquired through practice. The more often teachers have students write for myriad purposes, the more tools students have in their repertoire for learning. Content-area teachers do not need to *teach* students to write, per se. That is the job of the English Language Arts (ELA) teacher. However, content-area teachers can show students how to write as means to learn the more challenging content they will encounter as they move through the grades.

Of course, there is already some writing is incorporated into science classes now, for example, science journals or reports. But writing in science could be so much more valuable to students were we to show them how to use writing to develop ideas, thoughts, and perspectives about a topic in their content areas of study. With just a little effort and time, students can be taught to use writing to process and extend their thinking. They can personalize knowledge, information, and skills by using writing as a way to make connections between science and their own lives.

Science instruction could be so much richer were students empowered to use writing as a means to learn, rather than as an end in itself. It's time for writing to break free of its lonely 50-, 40-, 30-, or 20-minute scheduled block and be put to use helping students learn science.

WRITING IN THE SCIENCE CLASSROOM

The ultimate goal of any science class is to have students communicate their thinking, rationale, or understanding of subject matter. To communicate learning, you may already engage your students with myriad writing opportunities and not even realize it. This list is just a sampling of activities in which your students may write as a natural part of their everyday science instruction.

WRITING IN SCIENCE ACTIVITIES	
brainstorming	classifying
listing	comparing
webbing	describing
predicting	explaining
recording data	summarizing
analyzing data	note-taking
outlining	justifying

Writing helps students to become proficient with the concepts, skills, and topics in any science study. They can use writing to help clarify their ideas, record their thinking, internalize their learning, respond to learning, share their ideas, and gain thoughtful feedback to reflect on and adjust their ideas. Writing is a very personal act. Allowing students to engage in writing activities *daily* can only serve to strengthen their understanding of what can often be challenging and sometimes confusing content. And it need not take additional instructional time if it is considered an integral part of an everyday science routine. It's that important.

If you are like most science teachers, you don't consider yourself a writing teacher. That's fine. No one will be asking you to publish articles in—or guarantee your students are ready to write for—scientific journals. But remember that writing is a valuable learning tool, and it can be used quite effectively—and easily—to help students learn science content. Any topic in science can incorporate writing to support students as they research, keep data, record observations, create timelines, and keep personal notes to help them achieve this end.

INCLUDE WRITING AS A PART OF YOUR INSTRUCTIONAL PLAN

Here are some basics to accomplish integrating writing into your classroom day.

1. **Commit to incorporating writing *every day*.** Hopefully, you will see that writing in science is not complex or daunting. It can be, if an assignment includes multiple steps or outside research and composition. However, writing in science can also be as simple as generating a quick list (see p. 11), or summarizing information on a sticky note to post on a class chart (see p. 53). Regardless of the simplicity or complexity of the task, commit to writing in science every day.

2. **Provide models of writing in science.** Students accept their responsibilities better when they see the value and importance of their work as demonstrated by others. Read science-related articles from student-centered journals and magazines such as *National Geographic for Kids* or *Discovery Kids Online*. Even your local newspaper may have a special write-up about a science-related

topic now and again. Certainly, every community has ecological or geological concerns that the press is more than happy to share with its concerned citizens. Use these resources to enhance your instruction. (Be sure to follow up each reading selection with a writing activity. See Chapter 5.)

3. **Make sure every student keeps a science journal or a science log.** This can be a file, notebook, or concept folder for a particular unit of study. Chapter 1 addresses how to incorporate journaling into your science routine.

4. **Allow students to listen to and respond to each other's work.** Some written work, such as personal reflections and opinions, is completed for the sake of the person writing. Other writing, however, such as research and reporting, is meant to be shared. Students can sometimes be their own best teachers. Build a collaborative classroom community by allowing students to periodically share their written ideas with the class. Allow students' perceptions and ideas to be used as sounding boards for small group or class discussion or debate. This empowers students to be responsible for their own thinking, and they see that their written ideas are valued and appreciated. Many of the directions for each strategy in this book suggest paired or small group collaboration to complete a writing task, or they suggest providing time for students to share their work.

5. **Keep and maintain a science word wall or class learning wall.** Posting related science terms is okay. Building students' working vocabulary by displaying terms, definitions, examples, non-examples, and illustrations is better. Another option is to reserve classroom wall space for evidence of students' science learning. This can be accomplished by posting written work, diagrams, models, and illustrations of concepts the students have created. Whatever your students write, get it up where they can see it.

INSTRUCTIONAL BASICS FOR INTEGRATING WRITING

Once you have established the overall instructional climate, consider how to incorporate the following objectives for writing.

1. **Set a purpose for the written task.** Know why you are having students do what they are doing. Be sure students know why they are doing what they are doing. If it is just busy work, such as copying words and definitions, copying your notes, or writing down what you tell them to write, the purpose can only be "to study for the test." These are very un-engaging tasks, and they do not promote "writing." Instead, use writing to develop students' critical thinking skills, help them elaborate on known ideas, and generate individual definitions and summaries that make sense to them. It's their learning. Writing is a tool that allows them to own their learning.

2. **Make time.** Know how much time you want to devote to each writing strategy. Some student writing requires just a few minutes; others require whole or partial class periods. When students have not written at all during an entire

class period, at the very least stop class five minutes early to allow students to write or respond in their science journals. Don't think of this as lost instructional time; think of this as gained learning time.

3. **Set clear expectations.** Be sure students know what will happen to each writing task before they put pencil to paper. Perhaps what they write today will open the class discussion tomorrow.

4. **Model for and monitor students.** When students write in their science journals, you write in your science journal. When students are writing to contribute to the class, first do one class example. Then, walk the room. Let students know this is an important assignment.

5. **What if students can't or won't write?** Writing in science is an opportunity to organize ideas and summarize learning. Don't battle students' refusals. Instead, encourage and support students as needed. Most of the suggestions in this book are not lengthy writing tasks. Help students realize that a little time spent writing will help them learn important concepts.

Oftentimes, struggling readers are also struggling writers. For English Language Learners (ELLs), writing can be the last communication tool that they master (the others being reading, speaking, and listening). Each strategy in this book offers suggestions for scaffolding writing or differentiating learning to help ELL and at-risk students benefit from writing in science, regardless of their writing skill level.

HOW THIS BOOK CAN HELP

Strategies for Writing in the Science Classroom focuses on how you can use writing to develop critical thinking skills and help develop a deeper understand of science concepts during all stages of widely accepted, major science instructional models. This book does not go into exhaustive detail about how to teach writing skills, such as organizing content, grammar and punctuation, or the use of specific writing skills like using transition words. It also does not review the key steps to the writing process, nor does it expect science teachers to follow them exclusively when assigning essays or position papers. Students already will be learning and practicing all those writing skills within the writing process as part of a comprehensive study in language arts.

Instead, this book capitalizes on the application of writing skills to help students organize the jumble of ideas they likely encounter in a unit of study. For example, when writing a position paper to explain whether they think chimpanzees are smart, students should be expected to use the writing skills they learned in language arts to compose a thoughtful, meaningful, and coherent essay in science class. These expectations would be evident in the evaluation criteria the science teacher uses when assessing student work. (See Chapter 9) In addition, students can also use cloze activities, lab record sheets, and graphic organizers to apply understanding of content-specific vocabulary; record data, observations, and results; and organize informational text respectively, all through the use of writing.

These simple, engaging, and higher-order strategies help you integrate writing during all stages of any major science instructional model. First, let's briefly review an effective science lesson model. Science teachers may use the 5E instructional model (Bybee, et.al., 2006) or the 7E instructional model (Eisenkraft, 2003), both known as the "Activity-Before-Content" or ABC strategy. The 5E model includes five stages in a sequence of teaching and learning science. The 7E model closely mirrors the 5E model, but it includes two additional learning stages—one at each end of the lesson plan (See Table 1).

Most of us learned to write lesson plans following the Madeline Hunter model (1982). This model has undergone several revisions over the years, and we may call different stages by different names. However, it essentially remains the same, as seen in the far right column of Table 2. The 5E approach closely matches the effective Hunter model in the following:

1. Sparking student interest in a topic;

2. Building background and schema before engaging in learning;

3. Using text and multimedia resources to guide learning;

4. Allowing students to apply their learning; and

5. Allowing students to demonstrate mastery of the topic.

Science Instructional Model Comparison	
5E	**7E**
	Elicit Prior Understandings
Engage	Engage
Explore	Explore
Explain	Explain
Elaborate	Elaborate
Evaluate	Evaluate
	Extend

Table 1: A COMPARISON OF THE 5E AND 7E INSTRUCTIONAL SCIENCE LESSON PLANNING MODELS

5E Model	Description of 5E Stage	Madeline Hunter Lesson Plan Model
Engage	Peaks students' interest; gets students personally involved; assesses prior knowledge	Objectives Standards Anticipatory Set
Explore	Gets students involved in learning; allows students to build their own understanding; in science, explorations or investigations	Input
Explain	Allows students to communicate what they have learned so far; in science, text or multimedia information	Modeling Checking for Understanding Guided Practice
Elaborate (or Extend)	Apply acquired knowledge and understandings to new situations; in science, unique situations where students may practice their new skill	Guided Practice Closure
Evaluate	Demonstration of student learning	Independent Practice

Table 2: 5E INSTRUCTIONAL SCIENCE MODEL ALIGNED WITH THE HUNTER LESSON PLAN

Table 2 shows how the 5E instructional model closely matches the Hunter model. All the stages to a 5E plan lend themselves to the use of integrated writing activities. Most of the ideas in this book are effective writing strategies—tasks students can utilize during the process of learning in any situation to help them think about, reflect upon, organize, and comprehend any topic in any subject. This book organizes these writing strategies following the 5E model, starting with ideas to use during the *engage* stage of learning and culminating with ideas to use to *evaluate* or *assess* student learning. Most strategies follow a similar format:

TEACHER TIP

A fortunate byproduct of integrating writing into the content areas is the application of critical reading strategies. These skills are not listed in this section, but rather with each specific writing strategy in the book.

1. Title

2. Integrated ELA standards

3. Description or summary of the strategy

4. Teacher directions

5. Explanation as to how to use the student activity page, if applicable

6. Differentiation strategies for ELL, at-risk, and accelerated students

7. Suggestions for integrating technology

Many of the strategies include student examples. These are intended to help you visualize what completed student work might look like. Additionally, they may serve as models for students to follow so that you may set clear expectations regarding their notes and summaries.

Writing Strategies in the Science Classroom gives you solid strategies to use at every stage of the science instructional model. You can use writing before they even begin learning about a new science concept (*engage* and *explore* activities). They will be able to use writing all throughout the learning process (*explain* activities) and write to apply their learning in unique situations (*elaborate* or *extend* activities). Additionally, you can *evaluate* student progress through a unit of study using both formative and summative writing strategies.

Some of the strategies in this resource require just a few minutes; others may be better achieved over several minutes, one whole class period, or as an outside assignment. Regardless of your comfort level with writing, the step-by-step directions, student examples, and differentiation ideas will be all you need to start students writing in science TODAY!

Correlations to Common Core English Language Arts Standards*

At the elementary level, the Common Core English Language Arts Standards set requirements for reading literature, reading informational text, the foundational skills of reading (print concepts at kindergarten and first grade, phonological awareness, phonics and word recognition, and fluency at kindergarten through fifth grade), writing, speaking and listening, and language.

The intermediate level standards (grades 6-12) include standards for reading literature, reading informational text, writing, speaking and listening, and language. The suggestions in this book mainly target the Common Core writing standards for grades 4-8, as illustrated in Table 3 below.

*These Common Core English Language Arts (ELA) Standards have been simplified to span a wider range of grade levels. For specific grade level standards related to *Reading: Informational Text*, *Writing*, and *Language*, visit **www.corestandards.org/the-standards/english-language-arts-standards**.

STRATEGY	5E STAGE(S) OF LEARNING	STANDARDS
Science Notebooks, Concept Folders	All	Write opinions or arguments on topics or texts to support claims with clear reasons and relevant evidence.
		Write informational/explanatory texts to examine a topic and convey ideas, concepts, and information through relevant content.
		Draw evidence from informational texts to support analysis, reflection, and research.
		Summarize or paraphrase information in notes and finished work.
		Integrate information presented in different media or formats as well as in words to develop a coherent understanding of a topic or issue.
		Write routinely over time for a range of discipline-specific topics.
Graphic Organizers	All	Determine the main idea(s) and key details of a text.
		Describe the relationship between scientific ideas or concepts, using language that pertains to time, sequence, and cause/effect.
		Determine the meanings of words and phrases in text.
		Identify real-world connections between words and their uses.
		Write routinely over time for a range of discipline-specific topics.

Table 3: A CORRELATION OF THE WRITING STRATEGIES IN THIS BOOK TO THE 5E STAGES OF LEARNING AND THE COMMON CORE STATE STANDARDS (CCSS)

STRATEGY	5E STAGE(S) OF LEARNING	STANDARDS
Opinion Statements	Engage	Write opinion pieces on topics or texts, supporting a point of view with clear reasons and relevant evidence. Write routinely over time for a range of discipline-specific topics.
Quick Lists	Engage	Recall relevant information from experiences; take notes on sources and sort evidence into provided categories. Write routinely over time for a range of discipline-specific topics.
K-W-L Chart	Engage	Recall relevant information from experiences; take notes on sources and sort evidence into provided categories. Write routinely over time for a range of discipline-specific topics.
Key Word Predictions	Engage	Use context as a clue to the meaning of a word of phrase. Use reference materials to determine or clarify the precise meaning of key words and phrases. Write routinely over time for a range of discipline-specific topics.
Writing to Complete Lab Reports	Explore/Elaborate	Write informational/explanatory texts to examine a topic and convey ideas, concepts, and information through relevant content. Conduct research to answer a question. Produce clear and coherent writing appropriate to task, purpose, and audience. Write routinely over time for a range of discipline-specific topics.
Writing to Conduct Data Analysis	Explore/Elaborate	Conduct research to answer a question. Produce clear and coherent writing appropriate to task, purpose, and audience. Write routinely over time for a range of discipline-specific topics.

Table 3 cont.: A CORRELATION OF THE WRITING STRATEGIES IN THIS BOOK TO THE 5E STAGES OF LEARNING AND THE COMMON CORE STATE STANDARDS (CCSS)

STRATEGY	5E STAGE(S) OF LEARNING	STANDARDS
Writing to Complete Investigations	Explore/Elaborate	Write informational/explanatory texts to examine a topic and convey ideas, concepts, and information through relevant content. Conduct research to answer a question. Produce clear and coherent writing appropriate to task, purpose, and audience. Write routinely over time for a range of discipline-specific topics.
Writing to Record Observations	Explore/Elaborate	Write informational/explanatory texts to examine a topic and convey ideas, concepts, and information through relevant content. Conduct research to answer a question. Write routinely over time for a range of discipline-specific topics.
Vocabulary Comparisons	Explain	Write informational/explanatory texts to examine a topic and convey ideas, concepts, and information through relevant content. Conduct research to answer a question. Write routinely over time for a range of discipline-specific topics.
Mapping Vocabulary Words	Explain	Determine the meanings of words and phrases in text. Identify real-world connections between words and their uses. Use precise, domain-specific vocabulary to inform or explain. Identify real-world connections between words and their uses. Write routinely over time for a range of discipline-specific topics.
Sentence Summaries	Explain	Use precise, domain-specific vocabulary to inform or explain. Use context as a clue to the meaning of a word or phrase. Write routinely over time for a range of discipline-specific topics.

Table 3 cont.: A CORRELATION OF THE WRITING STRATEGIES IN THIS BOOK TO THE 5E STAGES OF LEARNING AND THE COMMON CORE STATE STANDARDS (CCSS)

STRATEGY	5E STAGE(S) OF LEARNING	STANDARDS
Vocabulary Word Sort	Explain	Determine the meanings of words and phrases in text. Identify real-world connections between words and their uses. Use precise, domain-specific vocabulary to inform or explain. Recall relevant information from experiences; take notes on sources and sort evidence into provided categories. Write routinely over time for a range of discipline-specific topics.
Using Graphic Organizers	Explain	Determine the main idea(s) and key details of a text. Describe the relationship between scientific ideas or concepts, using language that pertains to time, sequence, and cause/effect. Determine the meanings of words and phrases in text. Identify real-world connections between words and their uses. Write routinely over time for a range of discipline-specific topics.
Writing to Preview Text	Explain	Use text features and search tools to locate information relevant to a given topic efficiently. Use information gained from illustrations and the words in a text to demonstrate understanding of the text. Analyze how a particular sentence, paragraph, chapter, or section contributes to the development of ideas. Write routinely over time for a range of discipline-specific topics.
Making Personal Connections	Explain	Describe the logical connection between particular sentences and paragraphs in a text. Compare and contrast the most important points and key details presented in two texts on the same topic. Write routinely over time for a range of discipline-specific topics.

Table 3 cont.: A CORRELATION OF THE WRITING STRATEGIES IN THIS BOOK TO THE 5E STAGES OF LEARNING AND THE COMMON CORE STATE STANDARDS (CCSS)

STRATEGY	5E STAGE(S) OF LEARNING	STANDARDS
Recording on Sticky Notes	Explain	Determine the main idea(s) and key details of a text. Summarize or paraphrase information in notes and finished work. Describe the relationship between scientific ideas or concepts, using language that pertains to time, sequence, and cause/effect. Write routinely over time for a range of discipline-specific topics.
Taking Video Notes	Explain	Summarize or paraphrase information in notes and finished work. Integrate information presented in different media or formats as well as in words to develop a coherent understanding of a topic or issue. Write routinely over time for a range of discipline-specific topics.
What Does This Mean to Me?	Explain	Distinguish their own point of view from that of the authors of a text. Write routinely over time for a range of discipline-specific topics.
Writing to Complete Projects, Problems, and Prompts	Elaborate	Write opinions or arguments on topics or texts to support claims with clear reasons and relevant evidence. Write informational/explanatory texts to examine a topic and convey ideas, concepts, and information through relevant content. Write narratives to develop real or imagined experiences or events using effective technique, descriptive details, and well-structured event sequences. Write routinely over time for a range of discipline-specific topics.
Outside Writing Investigations and Research Projects	Elaborate	Integrate information presented in different media or formats as well as in words to develop a coherent understanding of a topic or issue. Conduct research projects to answer a question, drawing on several sources and generating additional questions for further research and investigation. Write routinely over time for a range of discipline-specific topics.

Table 3 cont.: A CORRELATION OF THE WRITING STRATEGIES IN THIS BOOK TO THE 5E STAGES OF LEARNING AND THE COMMON CORE STATE STANDARDS (CCSS)

STRATEGY	5E STAGE(S) OF LEARNING	STANDARDS
STEM Activities: Writing for Science in the Real World	Elaborate	Integrate information presented in different media or formats as well as in words to develop a coherent understanding of a topic or issue. Conduct research projects to answer a question, drawing on several sources and generating additional, related, focused questions for further research and investigation. Write routinely over time for a range of discipline-specific topics.
Writing for the Purpose of Formative and Summative Assessments	Evaluate	Summarize or paraphrase information in notes and finished work. Use precise, domain-specific vocabulary to inform or explain. Ask and answer questions to demonstrate understanding of a text. Write routinely over time for a range of discipline-specific topics.
Project-based Outcomes	Evaluate	Produce writing appropriate to task, purpose, and audience. Write routinely over time for a range of discipline-specific topics.

Table 3 cont.: A CORRELATION OF THE WRITING STRATEGIES IN THIS BOOK TO THE 5E STAGES OF LEARNING AND THE COMMON CORE STATE STANDARDS (CCSS)

Correlations to Common Core English Language Arts Standards for Integrated Technology

Many of the strategies in this book include suggestions for integrating technology. This particular standard is listed in the Common Core ELA standards. It applies to many of the added technology suggestions, including these listed in Table 4.

APPLICATION	PAGE	STANDARD
Blog	9	Use technology to produce and publish writing as well as to interact and collaborate with others.
Wiki	18	
Twitter	54	
Podcast	67	
Online Research	67	
Create a Website	79	

Table 4: INTEGRATED TECHNOLOGY ACTIVITIES AND THEIR CORRELATION TO COMMON CORE ELA STANDARDS

Common Core Writing Standards for Literacy in Science and Technical Subjects

Finally, the Common Core Standards include Reading and Writing Standards for Literacy in Science and Technical Subjects for grades 6-12. Table 5 shows the Common Core Writing Standards for Literacy in Science and Technical Subjects for grades 6-8. Note their parallel nature to the ELA standards listed for specific activities in this book on the previous pages.

STANDARD NUMBER	STANDARD
1	Write arguments focused on discipline-specific content.
2	Write informative/explanatory texts, including the narration of historical events, scientific procedures/experiments, or technical processes.
3	Not applicable.
4	Produce clear and coherent writing in which the development, organization, and style are appropriate to task, purpose, and audience.
5	With some guidance and support from peers and adults, develop and strengthen writing as needed by planning, revising, editing, rewriting, or trying a new approach, focusing on how well purpose and audience have been addressed.
6	Use technology, including the Internet, to produce and publish writing and present the relationships between information and ideas clearly and efficiently.
7	Conduct short research projects to answer a question (including a self-generated question), drawing on several sources and generating additional related, focused questions that allow for multiple avenues of exploration.
8	Gather relevant information from multiple print and digital sources, using search terms effectively; assess the credibility and accuracy of each source; and quote or paraphrase the data and conclusions of others while avoiding plagiarism and following a standard format for citation.
9	Draw evidence from informational texts to support analysis reflection, and research.
10	Write routinely over extended time frames (time for reflection and revision) and shorter time frames (a single sitting or a day or two) for a range of discipline-specific tasks, purposes, and audiences.

Table 5: COMMON CORE STATE STANDARDS (CCSS), READING AND WRITING STANDARDS FOR LITERACY IN SCIENCE AND TECHNICAL SUBJECTS, GRADES 6-12.

CHAPTER ONE

Note-Taking in Science

Students do not come to science class with an innate instinct for how to take notes. As much as all teachers would like this to be true, it just isn't the case. Note-taking is a learned behavior. Research regarding note-taking (Marzano, 2001) indicates that notes *should* be a work in progress, *should* be used as study guides for tests, *should* be taken frequently, and *should not* be recorded verbatim or copied. Science teachers can help develop students' abilities to take notes in class by utilizing one or more of the strategies described in this chapter: maintaining science notebooks, maintaining concept folders, or allowing students to record information using graphic organizers.

STRATEGY 1: SCIENCE NOTEBOOKS

Writers' notebooks are a safe place for writers to grow ideas for the writing craft. Science notebooks can be a parallel form of these, a continuous record written by students for themselves housing thoughts, ideas, and information before, during, and after learning. They have many benefits for students, including:

- Students can record their thoughts as they think like scientists.

- Students can record personal ideas related to concepts.

- Students can record observations to reflect on at a future date.

- Students can communicate using science-related terms.

- Students can strengthen their overall language and communication skills.

- Students can use the information they recorded to reflect on previous learning, and refine and strengthen current understanding.

- Students can save paper, since they can record ideas in one location versus on a variety of handouts.

- Students can use them as models for other disciplines, strengthening their overall study skills.

Science notebooks do not need to be fancy concept folders or costly investments. Instead, spiral-bound notebooks or composition books work just fine. Teachers can bring more meaning to their importance by allowing students to personalize their notebooks in some way (related to science, of course). Then, as students begin a new unit (see Chapters 2-3), read and learn about a particular concept or topic (see Chapters 4-6), extend their knowledge (see Chapter 7), and demonstrate their understanding (see Chapter 8), their notebooks provide a safe, personal, and meaningful place to record ideas and information, refine their understandings, and reflect on their learning. By the end of a unit of study, students will have a cohesive, complete, and meaningful compilation of their learning, demonstrating their deep understanding of the content.

The following tips will help students learn the value of maintaining their science notebooks. Likewise, teachers can use the students' notes as a record of learning before, during, and after a unit of study.

1. **Keep the science notebook close by.** One never knows when the mood to record information will strike. Writers are encouraged to keep their notebooks handy. Science students should keep their science notebooks accessible, too. For example, when learning about sound energy, students might become more "in tune" with the sounds around them. Having their notebooks at arms' length would allow students to instantly record their observations of the sounds around them. Then, when the time is right, they could refer to their observations and contribute more meaningfully to the class discussion. If the notebook is not at the ready, learners may miss recording their thoughts, which in turn will lose their personal connection to the content.

2. **Talk about it first.** The act of speaking is often easier than the act of writing. Adults and students alike oftentimes will turn to someone close by to discuss their ideas verbally before committing them to print. This is an effective strategy for ELLs and at-risk learners, too. Allow a little chat time before encouraging students to put pencil to paper.

3. **Allow students freedom of thought.** Copying from the board does not constitute note-taking. Introduce and teach ideas through exploration, video, observation, print, or any number of instructional strategies. Then, allow students to use their science notebooks to record their own thinking. The section in this chapter on the use of graphic organizers is one way to allow students to do this. Additionally, students can use thinking stems (McGregor, 2007) to record their own ideas related to any science concept or topic. Thinking stems are simply initial subject/predicate phrases that we use when reflecting upon our experiences or thoughts. They allow us to make personal connections to text, events, and information, making learning more meaningful (and memorable). (See **Figure 1.1.**)

I wonder... I see... I notice... I learned... I remember...

I know that _____ *, so* _____ *.*

Figure 1.1: SAMPLE THINKING STEMS

4. **Make time to write every day.** Every day? Yes, every day. Good writers write every day. Good science learners must internalize their thinking by making notes about the day's learning. Even a five minute commitment at the end of science class is satisfactory for students to think about what they learned, and record their ideas in their notebooks. Remember, notebooks are just one strategy for helping students learn their science content. If notebooks are not your forte, try the idea of concept folders (see p. 3), or use any one of several strategies during the engage, explore, explain, elaborate, and evaluate stage of the lesson. Remember, in order for writing to be an effective strategy to help students learn in science, they must have ready access to their notes. A science notebook is a convenient place to house information the students learn through writing.

Food for Thought

Will you grade student notes? Before making this decision, weigh the cost-benefit. On one hand, students who do not typically do well on tests can use their participation through writing to help improve their grades. On the other hand, a notebook is evidence of the *process* of learning, not the learning outcome per se. Some would argue that teachers are unfair to grade students as they practice learning. Involve your students in this decision. Decide ahead of time, as a class, whether this work will contribute toward their grade, and by how much: Ten percent? Fifty percent? What does that look like? Is a complete notebook worth one hundred points, and a partial notebook worth fifty points? Chapter 8 may help organize these ideas and help you and your students reach a suitable, equitable agreement regarding their written work and its role in their overall grade.

STRATEGY 2: CONCEPT FOLDERS

Concept folders are mini-notebooks that allow students to organize information in a variety of formats. Generally, they are made with folded and/or cut paper or paper products (such as paper bags) and have flaps, mini-pages, or hidden compartments. They may also contain one or two sheets of folded paper to make several pages, which students can use to take notes. A three-pronged pocket folder would also suffice as a simple concept folder.

Regardless of their shape or size, these carry-alls provide students with a place to store all their science work (labs, notes, vocabulary, etc.) in one convenient location for the duration of an entire unit of study. For example, if students are learning about different forms of energy, they could create a concept folder or pocket folder just for this unit. Then, as they conduct activities, investigations, and lab experiments; read and write about their personal connections to each form of energy; and summarize their learning, the students have a compilation of their work all in one place. At the end of the unit, students could remove all their work to take home, the teacher could store some or all of it as portfolio evidence, or the students could keep everything together for this unit and create a new folder for the next unit.

Concept folders should have all the same components as a science notebook, including blank or lined paper for students to record original and personal thoughts and ideas. The difference is that notebooks only have room to write. Additional information, such as student activity pages and vocabulary cards, should be stuffed inside the notebook pages or somehow stapled in. With concept folders, if students complete a lab sheet, a copy of this could be stored in one of the pockets. If the students keep their vocabulary words on note cards (for studying purposes), they could keep these in another pocket. Every piece of written work related to a particular topic should have its place in the concept folder or pocket folder.

TEACHER TIP

For project ideas to store student learning, try Amazing Hands-on Literature Projects for Secondary Students *by Deirdre Godin, or any one of a number of teacher resources from "The Bag Ladies" (Karen Simmons and Cindy Guinn) such as* A Bookbag of the Bag Ladies' Best, *all available from Maupin House Publishing.*

What It Looks Like

Figure 1.2 shows an example of a fourth grade student's Sound Journal science notebook. It was made using a brown lunch bag, cut and folded notebook paper, and a rubber band. Students made daily entries before, during, and after investigations. They also defined and illustrated related vocabulary terms, and summarized their learning at the end of the unit. **Figure 1.3** shows how to assemble this concept folder.

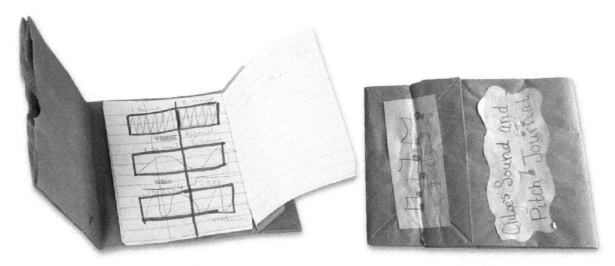

Figure 1.2: An example of a student's Sound Journal

To make a lunch bag folder, cut regular notebook paper in half to measure 8 x 5 ¼ inches. Stack several sheets together, then fold them in half (4 x 5 ¼ inches). Insert the fold of the notebook paper into the bottom flap of the lunch bag. Open the pages to the center of the notebook paper. Cut small slits (half an inch or so) down the folds of both the notebook paper and the bag. Place a rubber band around the bag and paper. It should wrap through the center of the notebook paper and fit into the slits. Fold the paper and the bag bottom to lay flat. Fold the top of the lunch bag to cover the notebook paper. Tuck it inside the bottom flap. Voilà! Your students have a portable, mini-notebook that is perfect for small note-taking tasks.

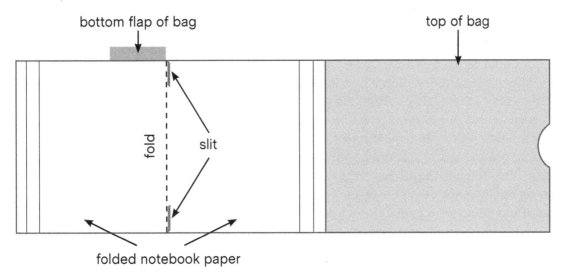

Figure 1.3: Illustration of the construction of a lunch bag notebook

Figure 1.4 shows an example of a science notebook for an eighth grade unit on ecosystems. Students kept notes, thoughts, and ideas in the center notebook pages. They stored lab reports, printed informational texts, and vocabulary cards in the pockets. At the end of the unit, students had a complete synopsis of the work they had done and the learning they accomplished. This notebook also provided students with a study guide for the end-of-unit test.

Figure 1.5 shows folded notes from a unit about stars. After learning about different types of stars, students folded a cut sheet of construction paper into four sections, labeled each section with a different type of star, and listed details about each type.

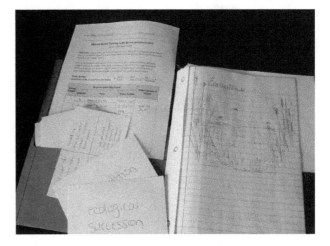

Figure 1.4: An example of a completed pocket folder science notebook

Figure 1.5: An example of folded notes from a unit about stars.

STRATEGY 3: GRAPHIC ORGANIZERS

Graphic organizers for general use are not restricted to reading class. In fact, they are powerful note-taking tools that students can use for any number of learning experiences in any context. They are particularly helpful and useful as students begin to develop an understanding of a multitude of concepts within a specific topic. For example, students learning about the three types of fault lines can use a tree diagram to explain each type and include an illustration (see **Figure 1.6**). Students can use a triple Venn diagram to compare the three types of muscles (see **Figure 1.7**). A sequencing organizer is perfect any time students need to record a process or cycle, such as the nitrogen cycle (see **Figure 1.8**). Really, at any point during the 5E process, students can use pre-printed or student-generated graphic organizers to suit any topic and any comprehension skill. The use of graphic organizers is a highly effective note-taking strategy, so they deserve mentioning here. Graphic organizers are discussed further in Chapter 5 during the *Explain* stage of the 5E science plan.

Adapting to Student Needs

Most graphic organizers are easy to replicate in a science notebook. For students who are capable of this task, show them a model or outline showing which layout they should use. For students who may have difficulty with this task, provide pre-printed organizers to complete and keep in a pocket folder. If necessary, further differentiate the use of the graphic organizer by completing some of the details, reducing the quantity of work necessary to complete the task.

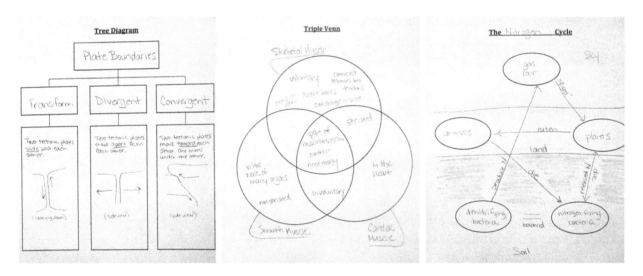

Figures 1.6, 1.7, and 1.8: EXAMPLES OF GRAPHIC ORGANIZERS USED DURING SCIENCE LEARNING

CHAPTER TWO

Writing to *Engage* Students

The first stage of the 5E instructional model in science is to engage students with the content. Typically, this is a brief activity designed to get their attention and start them thinking scientifically (wondering, asking questions, etc.). It also generates interest in the upcoming topic.

Effective engage activities include showing a short video, conducting a teacher demonstration, posing a thoughtful question, or showing a picture to generate conversation, to name a few. Regardless of the initial activity, the writing strategies in this chapter will provide the needed follow-up by allowing students to record their initial ideas, impressions, and opinions regarding the upcoming unit.

Strategy 1: Opinion Statements

Integrated English Language Arts Skills: Activating Prior Knowledge; Text-to-World Connections; Persuasion; Point of View

Summary: One way to grab students' attention when starting a new unit of study is to pose a philosophical question about a current event—a question that requires students to pull from their personal knowledge and analyze their own opinions.

Directions:

1. Enlarge the "What Do You Think?" learning template on p. 10 so that it is poster-sized. Write a yes or no question at the top. The question should elicit an opinion from the students, requiring them to establish a position on one side of the issue or the other.

2. Poll the students. Record the results on the template.

3. Have students discuss their positions in small groups or as a class.

4. Have students list the pros and cons for each side of the debate and write them down individually on sticky notes. Post each idea to the chart in the proper column.

5. Revisit this chart after the unit of study. Re-poll the class. Discuss whether students changed their position, and why.

What It Looks Like

Figure 2.1 shows how a class initially viewed the repeal of Pluto's planetary status. This question was posed to gain students' interest of current events related to our solar system, and then they learned about the specific planets.

Should Pluto be re-introduced as a planet? Yes: <u>16</u> No: <u>8</u>	
PROS	**CONS**
Many science textbooks are now wrong.	It doesn't clear its own orbit.
I had to make up a new mnemonic device to remember the order: My Very Energetic Mother Just Served Us Nine . . . ?	We would have to introduce a whole bunch more planets if we let Pluto back in because they all behave like Pluto.
It's been a planet so long, why change?	It's just a big rock in space.
It orbits the sun, like all the other planets.	Neptune doesn't clear its own orbit, either, so it should be taken off the list, too.

Figure 2.1: A SAMPLE CHART COMPARING STUDENTS' VIEWPOINTS

Other examples of effective questions include:

- Should the United States government require all citizens to get a seasonal flu shot?

- Are chimpanzees smart?

- Should the United States government continue to fund space exploration?

- Should one-half of our energy come from alternative sources, such as solar and wind?

- Is it every person's responsibility to reduce, reuse, and recycle?

- Should all nuclear energy sites be shut down?

- Should all new vehicles in production be electric?

Adapting to Student Needs

English Language Learners (ELLs) and at-risk students benefit from being able to discuss their ideas in a small group before sharing ideas with the class. They can also write a simple sentence or illustration on their sticky note, or have their idea transcribed for them by a peer.

Following the conclusion of the poll, accelerated students can conduct research about the question posed and report back to the class as the unit progresses. This adds students' personal involvement to the information presented, and adds to the efficacy of all students' abilities to make informed decisions based on facts and knowledge.

Adding Technology

If you have a blog, include the question the students are answering to it. Elicit responses from your colleagues and your students' friends and families. Discuss the going consensus and why people may be responding this way. As students move into the *explain* stage of learning, discuss how the research and information they read supports or refutes either or both sides to the debate.

WHAT'S A BLOG?

A blog is kind of like a place to post public journal entries. You can add comments, web links, images, media objects, and/or data to a continuous, chronological list of postings. Everyone has access to view everyone else's ideas. Many blogs turn into debating platforms. People have their opinions, and some are quite happy to share them with the world! A word of caution: some blog platforms restrict access, so not everyone can join in.

FREE BLOGGING WEBSITES

BLOGGER
www.blogger.com

TUMBLR
www.tumblr.com

WordPress
www.wordpress.com

What Do You Think?

Question: _____

_____

Yes: _____   No: _____

PROS	CONS

Strategy 2: Quick Lists

Integrated English Language Arts Skills: Main Idea & Details; Text-to-Self Connections; Brainstorming

Summary: Brainstorming is a simple yet effective way to get students' minds focused on an upcoming topic. Generating lists of related ideas is one brainstorming strategy in which nearly all students can participate. Also, these lists provide a "home base" to refer back to once learning is underway. The lists can be organized, sorted, categorized, and added to as learning progresses through the 5 E's. And, if you decide to have students complete a more comprehensive essay or other composition, these lists can act as a catalyst for the development of a topic statement.

Directions:

1. Post a topic/concept on a chart or on the board.

2. Place students with a partner. Give each pair a piece of scrap paper or a small whiteboard and a dry erase marker.

3. Allow them just thirty seconds to brainstorm as many words as they can that relate to the topic or concept.

4. Have students share their lists as a class. Record their ideas on the chart. As one group shares, the others listen and cross off the same ideas that appear on their lists. Continue to share as a class until all students' ideas are on the chart.

5. Use the student-generated list to guide instruction.

What It Looks Like

Figure 2.2 shows an abbreviated list of animals that was generated before beginning a unit related to animal adaptations and their habitats. Following their brainstorming session, students chose the two animals they believed were the most different. They completed a Venn diagram detailing how they knew the animals differed (including unique features and where they lived). As the students progressed through the *exploration* and *explanation* stages of the 5E model, they referred to this list to extend their thinking by adding additional animals that were not included during this initial activity.

ANIMALS OF THE WORLD				
giraffe	skunk	tortoise	gecko	dog
porcupine	donkey	dolphin	rat	butterfly
snake	sheep	toucan	elephant	lion
penguin	kangaroo	koala	bat	spider
tuna	whale	panda	centipede	buffalo

Figure 2.2: An abbreviated brainstorming list

Adapting to Student Needs

For beginning ELLs and at-risk students, allow them to use picture dictionaries to find examples related to a particular topic. They may also expand their own vocabularies by adding related words (such as the ones above) to a personal dictionary, which may double as a science journal. Use visuals of each sub-topic as often as possible, and allow students to work with a partner to encourage regular participation.

Accelerated students can categorize the class list. Provide them with additional chart paper and colored markers. Allow them to list the animals using categories: mammals, insects, reptiles, amphibians, fish, etc. (Students might include an "other" category for animals that don't fit the common classifications.)

Adding Technology

Use application software such as Kidspiration® or Inspiration® to allow students to categorize the animals from the lists they generate. For example, the animals listed might be categorized by the type of animal (i.e., bird, fish, insect, reptile, etc.), habitat (ocean, mountain, desert, arctic region, etc.), or characteristics (flies, swims, walks, etc.).

For information about this software, visit the Inspiration website, **www.inspiration.com**.

Additionally, Microsoft Word provides a bank of graphic organizers that students can insert within a word processing document. This "Smart Art" includes organizers for lists, processes, sequencing, cycles, and others.

Strategy 3: The K-W-L Chart

Integrated English Language Arts Skills: Activating Prior Knowledge; Text-to-Self, Text-to-Text, and Text-to-World Connections

Summary: Just as readers use prior knowledge to make meaning of new text, new science learning best takes place when students reflect on what they already know about a topic or concept. Before beginning a new unit of study, teachers can help students activate prior knowledge with the tried-and-true K-W-L chart (What I <u>K</u>now; What I <u>W</u>ant to Know; and What I <u>L</u>earned).

Directions:

1. Enlarge the K-W-L learning template on p. 16 so that it is poster-size. Write the topic of a current unit of study at the top.

2. Provide each small group of students its own copy of the K-W-L learning template on p. 16. The teams designate one person as the "recorder" and another person as the "sharer." Have students work collaboratively to discuss what they already know (or think they know) about this topic in the "K" column. The recorder writes the groups' ideas in the "K" column.

3. Have groups share what they know as a class. As the sharers report out, post each idea to the class K-W-L chart, regardless of whether the information is correct or incorrect. As the groups share, the other groups listen and cross out duplicate ideas.

4. As students list what they know about the topic, record any follow-up questions in the "W" column. Questions may arise from the students. However, this is an ideal opportunity to model a think-aloud strategy using questioning stems (see Figure 1.1). For example, if students are listing what they know about force and motion, ask them why water remains level no matter which direction the container turns. Post the question, "Why does water always remain level?" in the "W" column. Or, if students are listing what they know about animal adaptations, think aloud to yourself, "I wonder if a polar bear could live in the desert?" and post this question in the "W" column.

5. Finally, after the unit of study, return to the class K-W-L chart. Work as a class to circle the information the students confirmed as true, cross out the information they discovered to be false, and place a question mark beside information they did not confirm. Write statements about what the students learned in the "L" column.

6. Students may use one of the questions from the "W" column to explain what they learned in their science notebooks. (See Chapter 1 regarding the use of science notebooks.)

TEACHER TIP

Laminate the class poster and student copies of the K-W-L. Use dry erase markers to record ideas. Erase them when finished, and recollect them for another day.

What It Looks Like

Figure 2.3 shows a class K-W-L chart was completed during a unit about stars in our universe. All ideas were listed in the "K" column at the start of the unit, regardless of whether they were correct. Questions were written in the "W" column when students challenged others' facts. At the end of the unit, the class analyzed their initial ideas, circling the facts they confirmed, crossing out facts they learned were incorrect, and adding details in the "L" column.

ALL ABOUT STARS		
K	**W**	**L**
(Stars give off light.) ? (Stars are like fire.) (Stars are far away.) (Some stars are smaller than others.) (Some stars are brighter than others.) (They look like they blink.) (The sun is a star.) ~~The moon is a star.~~ ~~Stars can only be seen at night.~~	Are all stars the same size? Are all stars the same brightness? Are all stars the same age? Is the moon a star? Is the sun a star? Why do some stars look brighter than others?	Stars are different colors. The sun is a yellow star. Red dwarfs are the smallest stars. They are the most common, but you can't see them from Earth. Super giants are the largest stars. They are also the hottest. They explode into a supernova. Stars that are closer to Earth may appear larger, but they may be the same size as other stars that look smaller. Their distance from Earth just makes their size seem to change.

Figure 2.3: SAMPLE K-W-L CHART

Adapting to Student Needs

Once the teacher models the organizer effectively, students may begin to complete their own K-W-L charts in their science notebooks. Pair ELL and at-risk students, if needed, so they continue to learn from others. This also ensures that all students are engaged in the pre-learning activity. Likewise, all students can practice their listening and speaking skills, two additional essential communication skills.

Accelerated students can conduct independent research to answer questions in the "W" column that are not addressed during the unit. Have them create a suitable presentation (poster, slide show, or oral summary, for example), and set aside time for them to share their findings with the class.

Adding Technology

- Save a template of the K-W-L chart as an editable computer file. Type the day's topic at the top and post the chart to a Smart Board or other interactive whiteboard. Instead of a laminated chart, students can list their ideas on paper, or use their own electronic learning pads to record their ideas. Then, transfer the students' ideas to the digital class chart. Use the "save as" feature to save the file with the topic name, allowing this chart to be accessed throughout the learning process. This will also provide an electronic record of your learning as the year progresses.

- To complete step five in the directions, take a digital picture of the class chart. Print it on copy paper for each small group of students. Allow them to work collaboratively to circle confirmed information in the "K" column, cross out untrue information, and place a question mark beside unconfirmed information. They may also discuss the questions they posed in the "W" column, and list information they learned in the "L" column. Compare the groups' notes as a class. Discover whether the class uncovers any discrepancy in their learning. Use this opportunity to clarify any information, if needed.

K-W-L

Topic: _____

K	W	L

Strategy 4: Key Word Predictions

Integrated English Language Arts Skills: Context Clues; Vocabulary Development; Compare and Contrast

Summary: Some science concepts are quite challenging for students. For example, students may readily comprehend Earth science studies, yet struggle with chemistry or molecular science concepts. This strategy allows students to think ahead about what might be a challenging concept, reflect on the use of a term in context, and begin to assimilate their own definition of the term before learning related concepts and reading about complex details.

Directions:

1. Write an essential or key term in the indicated line on the Key Word Predictions template on p. 19. Write one or two sentences from a text source using this word in context, or create your own sentence(s). The sentence(s) should provide enough information for students to attempt to figure out what the word means.

2. Provide each student with a copy of the completed Key Word Predictions template. Have students independently read and reflect on the key word or phrase, and sentence(s). Then, they should write what they think the word means in the first column.

3. Have students work with partners to share their definitions with each other. They should write their partners' definition in the second column.

4. As a class, ask three or four students share their ideas. Use the class ideas to generate a class definition of the word. Or, use a glossary or dictionary to read the "official" definition. Record this class or text definition on the board for students to copy in the third column on their paper.

5. If desired, have students work with their partners to compare all three definitions: theirs, their partners', and the class'.

6. During the *explain* stage of the unit, have students reflect back on their initial ideas about this concept. Allow them to record their final understanding of this concept in their science journals.

What It Looks Like

Figure 2.4 shows an example of a key word prediction for the concept of *cell division*. The sentences do not define the term. Instead, the sentences provide information for students to begin to understand what cell division is, and why it happens. Related terms such as *mitosis*, *interphase*, *prophase*, *metaphase*, *anaphase*, and *telophase* will be easier to understand once students have a clear and comprehensive understanding of *cell division* by using this key word prediction strategy.

TERM:	Cell Division	
SENTENCE:	Cell division allows living things to grow larger. It also helps living things replace injured or unusable cells.	

MY DEFINITION	MY PARTNER'S DEFINITION	CLASS OR GLOSSARY DEFINITION
Cells divide. There are more of them.	Cells make more cells.	The process by which cells divide to form new cells.

How these definitions compare: Our definitions were alike. When cells divide, they make more cells. It is also a process. When cells divide, one cell becomes two cells. This also means there are new cells. They kind of reproduce.

Figure 2.4: SAMPLE "KEY WORD PREDICTION" CHART

Adapting to Student Needs

To support ELL and at-risk students, provide illustrations to support text whenever possible. For the example above, you might show students illustrations explaining the process of cell division, or show a picture of a plant in various stages of growth and ask, "How does this plant grow?" Allow students to verbalize their ideas with you or a peer before committing them to print.

Accelerated students can provide real-life examples of the concept, either in writing or with visuals (pictures, models, or real-life examples), to share with the class. Post these examples around the room or on a bulletin board throughout the unit of study. Use the examples as reference points to support and extend learning.

Adding Technology

Create a class wiki for each major concept studied throughout the course of the school year. As students learn new information, they may add it to the wiki page. These pages will provide supplemental text and research support as students continue to build on previous knowledge and extend current knowledge. This is also a meaningful way to publish student work. Assign students to update the wiki on a rotating basis. Students will have an equal opportunity to apply their writing skills for the benefit of the class.

WHAT'S A WIKI?

*A wiki is a collaboratively constructed website or series of related Web pages that documents information about a topic or a number of topics. Anyone can add to, delete, or revise the pages in any way. Wikis can also restrict editing privileges. Ideally, only experts who have undisputed information post updates to the site, but if a wiki is open to anyone, anyone can change the content of the wiki page(s). Wikipedia (**www.wikipedia.org**) is the best-known example of a wiki.*

*To start your own wiki, visit **Wikispaces** at www.wikispaces.com or **Intodit** at www.intodit.com.*

Key Word Predictions

TERM: _____

SENTENCE: _____
_____

MY DEFINITION	MY PARTNER'S DEFINITION	CLASS OR GLOSSARY DEFINITION

How these definitions compare: _____
_____
_____
_____

CHAPTER THREE

Writing While *Exploring* Science

During the *explore* stage of a 5E lesson, students typically participate in hands-on activities, explorations, investigations, or experiments; or, they observe a teacher demonstration of an activity. They might also watch videos demonstrating other people engaged in a particular investigation, then be asked to stop and reflect on what they think will happen next, or to record and analyze a set of data. **Figure 3.1** lists several examples of meaningful exploration activities. Regardless of the actual exploration, students should be held accountable for their work by writing to think, record, and respond.

SAMPLE EXPLORATION ACTIVITIES			
predictions	labs	experiments	investigations
observations	data analysis	field work	research

Figure 3.1: EXAMPLES OF EXPLORATION ACTIVITIES

After the exploration is complete, students can record personal thoughts or ideas, or summarize their learning in their science notebooks. If students have folders, their exploration handouts and record sheets should be included here.

The templates on the following pages provide generic resources for teachers to use as students conduct their explorations. The templates include:

Strategy 1: Writing to Complete Lab Reports

Use the Lab Report template (see p. 23) to conduct an experiment, lab, or investigation.

Before distributing this handout to students, write the title/topic of the experiment, and list the materials the students need. Then, make one copy of the Lab Report template for each lab group.

Provide each lab group with a copy of the steps to follow to conduct the experiment, or project them so that everyone can see them. Walk students through the steps of the experiment. Explain how this should be recorded on the Lab Report. An example of a completed report is on p. 24. Students may use it as a model to complete their own.

Collect their Lab Reports as evidence of learning. Make a copy of each report for all the group's members to keep for reference. If desired, use the **Lab Report Rating Scale** on p. 80 to evaluate the group's work.

Strategy 2: Writing to Conduct Data Analysis

Use the Data Analysis template (see p. 25) when students collect data during a lab or investigation.

Students may need assistance setting up tables and charts to collect and organize their data. Provide models for students (such as the one on pp. 26-27), set up tables or charts as a class before conducting experiments, or conference with each lab group individually during the experiment. Be sure they have an appropriate format to use when collecting and recording data. For example, some data is best collected using tally marks, while other data is best collected on a table or in a list.

When students begin creating a graph to illustrate their data, be sure they know the expectations ahead of time. The example on p. 26-27 shows how students who completed the Ball Drop investigation might graph their results. Review this example with the class to provide a model for them as they organize their data into a readable graph. Review the evaluation criteria from the Data Analysis Rubric on p. 81 with students so they know how their data charts and graphs will be evaluated.

Strategy 3: Writing to Complete Investigations

Use the Investigations template (see p. 28) when involving students in any activity that is not strictly a lab.

For example, students might go on a "sound hunt" around the building, listening for and listing different sounds that they can later describe using the Observation Activity Sheet (p. 29). Perhaps students are participating in a geologic time or cell division activity that is more about discovery than experimentation. Another example of a non-lab activity is the construction of a model of a topic or process, such as the water cycle or ocean currents. Whatever the investigation, this template will keep students focused on the task and the objective and will provide a structured outline for them as they complete their work.

Collect their Investigation as evidence of learning. If students are working in lab groups, make a copy of the report for each group's members to keep as reference. If desired, use the **Lab Report Rating Scale** on p. 80 to evaluate student work.

Strategy 4: Writing to Record Observations

Use the Observation Activity Sheet on p. 29 to help students learn to organize their findings in a matrix. Science is all about making observations upon which to draw conclusions. A matrix allows students to record their observations when comparing different items with similar features across several categories.

For example, primary students might take measurements of three different peanuts in their shells. Students can number and list each peanut along the top row, and the measurements they take (length, circumference, and weight) along the left column. Alternatively, they can observe three different rocks or soil samples, observing their texture, color, and particles (see **Figure 3.2** below). Intermediate students might look at pictures from four different ecosystems. They can compare the producers, primary and secondary consumers, and decomposers that inhabit each ecosystem. Students can then conduct research to complete the chart with facts and information they cannot see in each picture, or continue to fill in information as the unit progresses. **Figure 3.3** shows an example of how a matrix with this information may be organized.

Have students keep their observation record sheet in their science notebooks to refer to as learning continues.

Characteristics	Soil Sample 1	Soil Sample 2	Soil Sample 3
Particles	very fine	mix of small and large	medium to large
Color	orange-ish brown	dark brown, almost black	light to medium brown
Texture	mostly dry and gritty	mushy	some grit, but mostly mushy

Figure 3.2: MATRIX ORGANIZING STUDENT OBSERVATIONS OF SOIL SAMPLES

Ecosystem	Inhabitants			
	Producer	Primary Consumer	Secondary Consumer	Decomposers
Wetland	Cattail, duckweed	Grasshoppers, deer	Alligators, snakes	Insect larvae, bacteria, fungi
Desert	cactus, wild flowers	rabbits, quail	snakes, coyotes	termites, fungi
Rainforest	Moss, ferns, trees	Grasshoppers, beetles, slugs	Wood-peckers, leopards	Termites, fungi, earthworms
Ocean	Phyto-plankton, algae	Zooplankton, sea turtles	Sharks, octopus, tuna	Marine worms, shrimp

Figure 3.3: MATRIX ORGANIZING STUDENT OBSERVATIONS OF ECOSYSTEMS

Lab Report

Experiment Title or Topic: _____

Date: _____ Class: _____

Name(s): _____

What are you investigating?: _____
_____
_____
_____

What do you think will happen?: _____
_____
_____
_____

List the materials you need to conduct this experiment:

_____   _____   _____
_____   _____   _____
_____   _____   _____

Summarize the steps you will follow to conduct this experiment: _____
_____
_____
_____
_____

After you have conducted the experiment, record your observations: _____
_____
_____
_____

Record your results. Create a chart on another sheet of paper, if needed: _____
_____
_____
_____

What conclusion(s) can you draw from this experiment?: _____
_____
_____
_____
_____

Lab Report *student example*

Experiment Title or Topic: Ball Drop

Date: October 16, 2011   Class: Third Period

Name(s): Rob, Kendra, Gigi, Faith

What are you investigating?: Does the height of a rubber ball affect the reaction force of the floor?

What do you think will happen?: The higher the ball, the greater reaction force.

List the materials you need to conduct this experiment:

rubber ball	tape
meter sticks x2	chair

Summarize the steps you will follow to conduct this experiment: We will hold the ball above the floor at .5 m, 1.0 m, 1.5 m, and 2.0 m. We will drop the ball from each height and record how high the ball bounces after its first bounce off the floor. We will repeat these steps three times.

After you have conducted the experiment, record your observations: The ball bounced fewer centimeters when dropped from the lowest point. The ball bounced more centimeters when dropped from the medium point. The ball bounced the most centimeters when dropped from the highest point.

Record your results. Create a chart on another sheet of paper, if needed:
See our data analysis sheet

What conclusion(s) can you draw from this experiment?: The higher the starting point of the ball, the greater the reaction force of the floor on the ball.

Data Analysis

Activity Title or Topic: _____

Date: _____ Class: _____

Name(s): _____

Why are you collecting data?: _____
_____
_____

Why is this important?: _____
_____
_____

1. Decide how you will collect data and circle all that apply:
   - Notebook paper
   - Graph paper
   - Plain paper
   - A chart or table
   - A list
   - Other _____

2. Collect your data. Be thorough, as this will be used to draw conclusions later.

3. Organize your data. Use another sheet of paper or a computer program. Make a chart or a graph. Be sure the graph matches the data, or simply reorganize your table so that it is neat and easy to read.
   - If you are comparing changes over time, create a line graph.
   - If you are comparing discrete data, make a bar chart or double bar chart.
   - If you want to compare parts to a whole, make a pie chart.

4. Analyze the data. Record your comparisons. Be clear—anyone who reads your summary should understand what the data is telling you.

_____
_____
_____

What conclusion(s) can you draw from this data?: _____
_____
_____
_____

How did collecting and organizing data help you learn more about this topic?:
_____
_____
_____

Data Analysis *student example*

Activity Title or Topic: *Ball Drop*

Date: *October 16, 2011*   Class: *Third Period*

Name(s): *Rob, Kendra, Gigi, Faith*

Why are you collecting data?: *We want to see if the reaction force of the floor changes when a ball is dropped from a higher place.*

Why is this important?: *If things are dropped, the height might change what happens to them when they hit the floor.*

1. Decide how you will collect data and circle all that apply:
    - Notebook paper   • Graph paper   • Plain paper
    - A chart or table   • A list   • Other _____

2. Collect your data. Be thorough, as this will be used to draw conclusions later.

3. Organize your data. Use another sheet of paper or a computer program. Make a chart or a graph. Be sure the graph matches the data, or simply reorganize your table so that it is neat and easy to read.
    - If you are comparing changes over time, create a line graph.
    - If you are comparing discrete data, make a bar chart or double bar chart.
    - If you want to compare parts to a whole, make a pie chart.

4. Analyze the data. Record your comparisons. Be clear—anyone who reads your summary should understand what the data is telling you.

The reaction force of the floor when a rubber ball is dropped on it changes when the starting height of the ball changes. When the ball is dropped from a lower place, the reaction force is low. When the ball is dropped from a higher place, the reaction force is high. We know this because the height of the ball's bounce was greater when dropped from a greater height.

What conclusion(s) can you draw from this data?: *The higher the bounce height, the greater the reaction force of the floor.*

How did collecting and organizing data help you learn more about this topic?:
When we put the data in a bar chart, we could compare the heights of each ball drop.

Data Analysis *student example, cont.*

Activity Title or Topic: **Ball Drop**

Date: **October 16, 2011**   Class: **Third Period**

Name(s): **Rob, Kendra, Gigi, Faith**

Table showing reaction force for each trial

	.5 meters	1.0 meters	1.5 meters	2.0 meters
Trial 1	38 cm	79 cm	109 cm	152 cm
Trial 2	39 cm	77 cm	104 cm	164 cm
Trial 3	40 cm	73 cm	110 cm	157 cm

Chart showing data in table

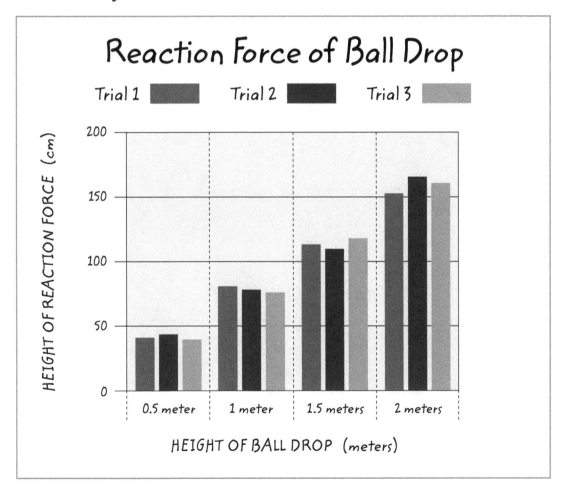

Investigation

Investigation Title or Topic: _____

Date: _____ Class: _____

Name(s): _____

What are you investigating?: _____
_____

What do you already know about this topic?: _____
_____
_____

What do you think you'll discover?: _____
_____

List the materials you need to conduct this investigation:

_____ _____ _____
_____ _____ _____
_____ _____ _____

Summarize the steps you will follow to conduct this investigation:
_____
_____
_____
_____

After you have conducted the investigation, record your observations:
_____
_____
_____
_____

What did you learn that you did not know before the investigation?:
_____
_____
_____
_____

What surprising or interesting information did you discover
while conducting this investigation?:
_____
_____
_____
_____

Observation Activity Sheet

Directions: Label each column with characteristics or qualities. Label each row with the objects or items you are observing. Make your observations. Describe each characteristic or quality in the right space.

OBJECTS OR ITEMS			
Characteristics or Qualities			
Characteristics or Qualities			
Characteristics or Qualities			
Characteristics or Qualities			

CHAPTER FOUR

Writing During Learning: *Explain—*
Developing Science Vocabulary

So far in the 5E science instructional plan, students have had the opportunity to engage with the content and explore on their own. The previous two chapters provided several strategies to have students use writing as a means to express their ideas and record their observations. Now, students move to learn the information that they could not necessarily discover through inquiry and activity. Most scientific information comes to students from textbooks, articles, and websites. But just as students do not come to science class knowing intrinsically how to take notes, they may not have had

QUICK TIP

One strategy for developing vocabulary, Key Word Predictions, can be found on p. 17 in Chapter 2.

adequate practice applying reading strategies to comprehend informational text. We read non-fiction much differently than we read fiction. First of all, we have a different purpose. Rather than reading for entertainment, we read non-fiction to gain knowledge. Everything about non-fiction text is different: the structure of the text, the structure of the sentences, and the vocabulary. They all work in a logical, informative manner to provide the information we seek.

Unfortunately, this type of literature can be boring, dry, and monotonous. Students without a passion to read about science or any particular topic within science will likely tune out, drift off, or simply not read their assignment. Although they may have participated in and learned something from the activity prior to this point, knowledge presented may stymie them unless you, the science teacher, provide adequate support for students to truly learn from the texts they read. The strategies in this chapter help students stay active readers from the first through the last word.

One component of reading that can directly impact students' comprehension of informational text is their ability to identify and understand essential vocabulary terms. For example, students who are reading about Earth's natural resources will not learn much if they do not have at least a basic understanding of the terms *resources, renewable, nonrenewable, fossil fuels, and geothermal* (to name a few). The likelihood of students having encountered these terms in fictional reading prior to their instruction in science class is minute.

As a science teacher, do not assume students come to class already knowing these words, or that they will pick them up naturally through content-area reading. Instead, students stand a much greater chance of learning and comprehending informational text when essential words are taught directly (Marzano, 2001). The following are four additional strategies to help students gain a working understanding of the scientific vocabulary they will encounter in text.

Strategy 1: Vocabulary Comparisons

Integrated English Language Arts Skills: Vocabulary Development; Compare and Contrast

Description: This strategy requires students to have a deep and thorough understanding of key terms. This strategy assumes students have had direct instruction with related terms and are ready to apply their understanding in a higher-level context.

Using the Template:

1. Print one copy of the Vocabulary Comparisons learning template on p. 33 for each student.

2. Read the directions and the example together.

3. Complete one example using a current term as a class, if needed.

4. Provide a list of items from which to make comparisons and insist that students choose from the list.

5. Have students keep a copy of their comparisons in their science notebooks.

6. As students become proficient developing comparisons, encourage them to think and record their own. Any comparison is acceptable as long as they justify it appropriately.

What It Looks Like

Figure 4.1 shows an example of how a student might make comparisons with terms from a unit on the properties of matter.

Density is like a _farm_ because _crops are packed really tight together, and others are more spread out._

An object's _boiling point_ is like a _camera_ because _the button can only take so much pressure (heat) before it snaps a picture (boils)._

Figure 4.1: SAMPLE VOCABULARY COMPARISONS

Adapting to Student Needs

If necessary, list the terms for ELL and at-risk students before copying the template. You might also provide a list of common ideas for them to choose from to make their comparisons. Students who cannot write could have their ideas transcribed for them, or they could be allowed to illustrate and label their ideas.

Another differentiation strategy is to pair students for this activity and have each pair share their ideas with another pair of students (called a "pair-share"). This increases students' verbal discussion of each term and provides peer support and collaboration for what can be a very challenging assignment.

Accelerated students can explain and illustrate their ideas on note cards. Post select examples on a word wall for students to refer to throughout the unit.

Adding Technology

Have one or two students create a spreadsheet listing each scientific term, and all the students' common ideas for each term. Print this page, enlarge it using a poster printer, and display it throughout the duration of the unit.

Alternatively, use an online poster-building website, such as Glogster (**www.edu.glogster.com**) to have students artfully type their comparisons.

Vocabulary Comparisons

Directions: Think about the meaning of each scientific term. Compare the term to a common idea. Explain how this term and the idea you listed are *alike*.

Example: <u>Invertebrates</u> are like <u>cowards</u> because <u>they have no backbone.</u>

TERM	COMMON IDEA	EXPLANATION

Strategy 2: Mapping Vocabulary Words

Integrated English Language Arts Skills: Vocabulary Development; Compare and Contrast

Description: Vocabulary mapping is a high-yield strategy (*Just Read Now*) that helps students learn essential terms in science or in any other content area. As with concept maps, the essential term takes center stage on the page. Then, students include four related components (a definition, illustration, original sentence, examples, non-examples, or characteristics) in each of four areas surrounding the term.

Using the Template:

1. Print one copy of the Vocabulary Maps learning template on p. 36 for each student. This template provides space for three terms. Make enough copies so that each student has adequate maps for each of his or her science terms.

2. Read the directions as a class.

3. Complete one example as a class using a current term, if necessary.

TEACHER TIP

Have students copy this template in their science notebooks—one template for each term—to eliminate the use of copies. Another option is to have students copy the template on note cards.

4. Have students keep a copy of their comparisons in their science notebooks.

Students can also make their own vocabulary map templates using folded paper:

- Fold a sheet of paper twice to make four quadrants.

- Fold the corner where both folds meet on a slight angle. This will make a triangle.

- Open the paper. Trace the folds with marker or colored pencils. The triangle fold should make a center square in the center of the page. Have students complete the template as shown on p. 36.

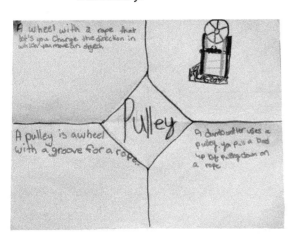

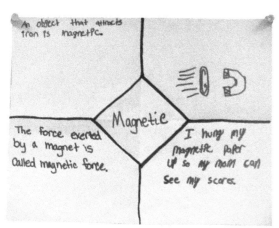

Figure 4.2: STUDENT EXAMPLES OF VOCABULARY MAPS USING FOLDED PAPER.

What It Looks Like

The vocabulary maps in **Figure 4.2** were completed using folded construction paper. Students can easily make one map for each term to keep in their science notebooks. These maps include a definition, illustration, example, and original sentence.

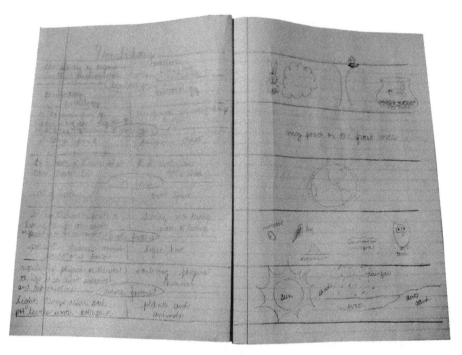

Figure 4.3 shows how a student might copy and complete the vocabulary template in his or her science notebook. This example also includes illustrations for each term, another highly effective vocabulary learning strategy (Marzano, 2001).

Figure 4.3: STUDENT EXAMPLE OF VOCABULARY MAPS IN A SCIENCE NOTEBOOK.

Adapting to Student Needs

Allow at-risk and ELL students to work in pairs or small groups to make their vocabulary maps. Instead of producing original sentences, have these students record the sentences that use each word from the text, or help them develop original sentences following a discussion of the words.

Accelerated students can create quiz cards for each term. Have them write the term on the front of a note card, and then create their quadrants on the back. Before administering a vocabulary quiz, have pairs or small groups of students use the cards to quiz each other.

Adding Technology

Create this template using a word processing program. Use the Shapes tools (iWork Pages) or SmartArt (Microsoft Word) functions to design and create your own template for students. Then this template can be emailed to students for them to complete either at school (if adequate computers are available) or at home.

If you have a Google account, you can create your template online via Google Docs (**www.google.com/google-d-s/tour1.html**) and then invite your students to log on and revise a single document online. Visit Google Apps for Education to learn more: **www.google.com/apps/intl/en/edu/k12.html**.

Vocabulary Maps

Directions: Write each term on the line in the center of the map. Write the definition in the upper left block. Write the characteristics of the term in the upper right block. List examples and non-examples in the lower grids.

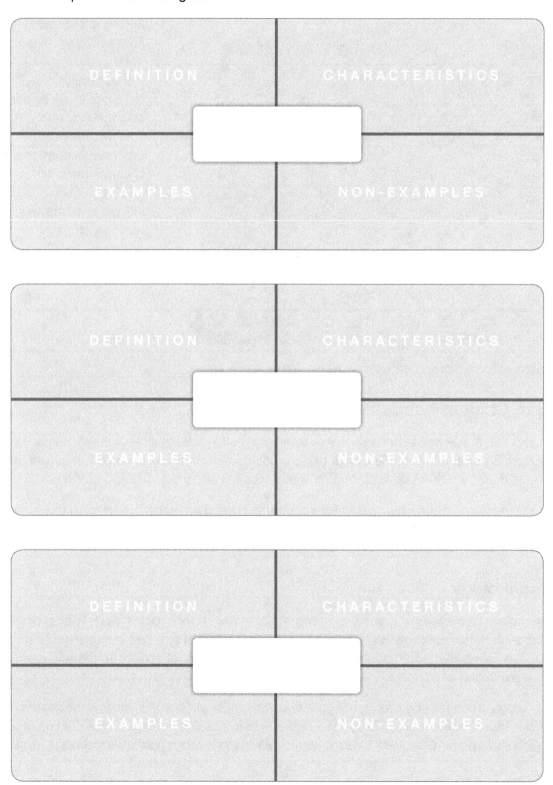

Strategy 3: Sentence Summaries

Integrated English Language Arts Skills: Vocabulary Development; Summarizing

Description: This strategy develops students' general language arts skills while simultaneously strengthening their understanding of essential vocabulary terms. Students write one of four different types of sentences (e.g., statement, question, exclamation, and command) using their vocabulary terms. Then, they pass their paper to add additional sentences using different terms. At the end of four rounds, students have one paper using four terms, each in an original sentence.

Using the Template:

1. Print one copy of the Sentence Summaries learning template on p. 40 for each student.

2. Read the directions together.

3. Post a list of vocabulary terms to review or allow students to have access to their science notebooks, which include the terms and definitions.

4. Set a short time limit, about thirty to sixty seconds. Have each student write one sentence on the paper. Students do not need to start at the top of the page. They may write any one of the four types of sentences using any of the vocabulary terms.

5. When time is up, have students fold their paper in half and pass it to the person on their right. Once everyone has a different piece of paper, start the clock again. Students should open their paper and write a new sentence to complete the page using a second vocabulary word. For example, if the person to his or her left wrote a command, the student may now write a statement, question, or exclamation using a different term than the one previously used.

6. Continue this for two more rounds, until all the sentences are complete. Then, have students pass their papers to the right once more. The fifth person opens the paper and independently reads all the sentences.

7. Have three or four students share a statement with the class, and then have three other students share a question. Follow this with three other students who share an exclamation and three others who share a command.

8. Collect the students' papers to use for assessment purposes (see Chapter 8).

What It Looks Like

You might see the sentences in **Figure 4.4** included on a paper during a unit about energy changes.

STATEMENT

The poster hanging on the wall has potential energy.

QUESTION

How much kinetic energy does a roller coaster have after it goes over the first hill?

COMMAND

Measure your energy using calories, not joules.

EXCLAMATION

I sure am tired from skiing down that hill, even though I know the law of conservation of energy says no energy was created or destroyed!

Figure 4.4: SENTENCE SUMMARY EXAMPLES

Adapting to Student Needs

Provide examples on the board of each type of sentence (see **Figure 4.5**). You may choose to allow students to work in pairs when applying this strategy for the first time in your classroom.

SENTENCE TYPES	
Statement:	A declaration that has a subject and predicate, usually in that order, and ends with a period (.)
Question:	An interrogative expression that ends with a question mark (?)
Command:	An expression that gives an order and ends with a period (.) or exclamation point (!)
Exclamation:	A sharp or sudden expression that ends with an exclamation point (!)

Figure 4.5: TYPES OF SENTENCES

Accelerated students can write extended sentences that include phrases, dialogue, hyperbole, onomatopoeia, or any number of creative writing strategies.

Adding Technology

Have one or two students type the sentences in a large font using a word processing program or on a poster in Glogster (**www.edu.glogster.com**). Print the sentences or posters, and then post them on a word wall throughout the unit of study.

Another option is to have students tweet their sentences. You can make a classroom Twitter account (**www.twitter.com**), and have students submit handwritten tweets (sentence summaries of 140 characters or less) each week. For example: *Measure your energy using CALORIES, not joules. #Command #EnergyChanges*

Sentence Summaries

Directions: Choose one of your vocabulary words. Decide whether to use your word in a statement, a question, a command, or an exclamation. Write your sentence on the lines in the correct space. Circle the vocabulary word you used. When time is up, pass this paper to your right. On the paper *you* are handed, look at what your neighbor previously wrote. Choose a different vocabulary word and write a different type of sentence with this second word. You will do this a total of four times.

STATEMENT

_____

_____

_____

QUESTION

_____

_____

_____

COMMAND

_____

_____

_____

EXCLAMATION

_____

_____

_____

Strategy 4: Vocabulary Word Sort

Integrated English Language Arts Skills: Vocabulary Development; Similarities and Differences

Description: Some science topics may have an abundance of related vocabulary terms, perhaps too many for students to learn within the given time frame of a particular unit. Marzano (2001) contends that, in order for vocabulary learning to be meaningful, students should be required to truly learn between five and seven critical terms and phrases from any particular unit of study. Within the context of teaching science, some topics are quite vocabulary-heavy, and students may be encountering these words for the first time.

This strategy encourages repeated exposure to related vocabulary terms, whether the teacher decides to directly instruct the words, or allows students to encounter them in context. Students work collaboratively to first sort the words into two, three, or four categories, and then write to explain why the words were sorted in this manner.

Directions:

1. Write each vocabulary word for a current topic or unit in its own space on the Vocabulary Word Sort learning template on p. 43.

2. Copy the words so that each pair or small group of students has one copy of the set.

3. Cut the words apart and place them in an envelope, clear zipper bag, or simply clip them together.

4. Have students work collaboratively with their group to discuss the words and sort them according to how they relate to each other. Leave the number of categories open. Students may sort the words into two sets, three sets, or even four sets. Groups may sort words using categories that differ from each other.

5. Have students summarize their sorting strategy in their science notebooks. Then, have one person from each group share with the class which words they placed together with justification.

What It Looks Like

Figure 4.6 shows how a group sorted words related to a unit about atoms. When the group was questioned about why they included ionic and covalent bonds in the "atoms" category, one student responded that those bonds are related to how the atoms share electrons, so they are more closely related to the "atoms" category than the "combination of atoms" category.

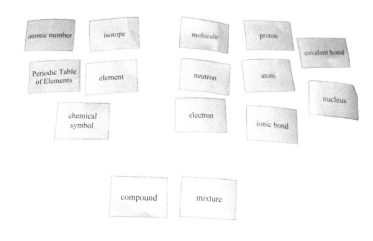

NOTEBOOK ENTRY

1. *Atoms: atom, proton, neutron, electron, molecule, nucleus, ionic bond, covalent bond. They all have to do with atoms or parts of atoms.*

2. *Combinations of atoms: mixture, compound. They both explain how atoms can combine.*

3. *Elements: element, atomic number, chemical symbol, isotope, and Periodic Table of Elements. They all have to do with elements.*

Figure 4.6: EXAMPLE OF SORTED VOCABULARY TERMS FROM A UNIT ABOUT ATOMS, AND A CORRESPONDING NOTEBOOK ENTRY JUSTIFYING EACH CATEGORY

Adapting to Student Needs

Provide at-risk and ELL students with pictures illustrating the vocabulary terms. Encourage collaboration from each group member throughout the sorting process.

Challenge accelerated students to sort, then resort the terms using different categories. Their science notebooks will then have two summaries to justify the relationship among the words for each sorting exercise.

Adding Technology

Create a PowerPoint slide listing all the terms, each in its own text box. Project the slide onto an interactive whiteboard, and then work as a class to sort the terms into categories. On a second slide, type a summary as a class. Print the slides, and post them on a learning wall throughout the unit of study.

An alternative is Scribblar (**www.scribblar.com**), a free, interactive whiteboard site.

Vocabulary Word Sort

Directions: Write your vocabulary words, one in each space. Cut the words apart. Sort them into categories. Place the words that are related into one category. Place other words that are related into a second category. You may have up to four categories. Summarize how you sorted the words. Use a sheet of paper. Explain why you sorted them this way.

CHAPTER FIVE

Writing During Learning: *Explain—*
Reading and Writing in Science

"... Proficient readers connect what they read to their own lives ... this type of reading promotes engagement and enhances understanding."

— STEPHANIE HARVEY, *Nonfiction Matters: Reading, Writing, and Research in Grades 3-8*

As discussed in the previous chapter, we read non-fiction with a different purpose than we read fiction. Stephanie Harvey (1998) writes that students (and adults alike) engage in non-fiction text to gain information, learn something new, develop a deeper understanding of prior knowledge, and to... have fun? Yes, non-fiction reading can be fun.

The strategies in Chapters 2 and 3 assume students begin their science understanding through activity first. Chapters 4 and 5 delve into how students develop deeper understanding through content-area reading. Chapter 4 focused on how students can use writing to learn essential vocabulary. This chapter provides writing strategies for students to make personal connections while reading informational text. Oftentimes, this content area reading comes to students through published textbooks. Teachers, especially those just beginning their careers, rely on published texts to provide students with the information they need to be successful in class and on statewide and national assessments.

In addition to published texts, students can also gain information through articles in science-related magazines such as *National Geographic for Kids* or *Time for Kids*, local or national newspaper articles, non-fiction books, online encyclopedias or other reliable electronic media, and a host of additional sources. There is a lot of information to read! Regardless of the text that students read to learn, the writing strategies in this chapter allow students to make personal connections with non-fiction literature to develop their science literacy.

Strategy 1: Using Graphic Organizers

Integrated English Language Arts Skills: Predicting; Brainstorming; Webbing; Main Idea and Details; Compare and Contrast; Cause and Effect; Vocabulary Development; Making Inferences; Drawing Conclusions; Fact and Opinion; Sequencing; Note Taking; and Summarizing

Description: The use of graphic organizers was first introduced in Chapter 1 as an effective note-taking strategy. This section serves as a reminder about their value and importance to help students sort, categorize, and comprehend a multitude of information during non-fiction reading. Additionally, graphic organizers serve as effective reviews of key concepts throughout a unit of study and as valuable study guides leading up to a summative assessment of the content.

Directions:

1. First, decide which literacy skill(s) to which the text lends itself, such as compare and contrast, sequencing, or main idea and details.

2. Provide a graphic organizer to match these skills. For example, if students are reading to find the main idea and related details of a particular text, give them a graphic organizer suited to record main ideas and details. If students are reading to compare two related ideas, give them a graphic organizer suited to this purpose.

Teachers have the option of printing graphic organizers for student use, or, after having completed similar organizers, students can copy the templates into their science notebooks to complete. Another option is to begin or complete a class organizer to post on a learning wall to reference throughout a unit of study. Regardless of the method of use, students should be encouraged to record information using graphic organizers to help them sort through and apply meaning to what can otherwise become overwhelming and mundane informational reading.

What It Looks Like

Figure 5.2 and **Figure 5.3** show two examples of graphic organizers, one for recording cause-and-effect relationships, and the other for listing facts and examples for three related topics. Three other examples may be found on p. 6.

Adapting to Student Needs

Consider students' abilities when deciding on the amount of information expected for each organizer's completion. For example, you may consider providing the main ideas for at-risk and ELL students, requiring them to only read and record the details. Or, consider reducing the number of details your at-risk and ELL students need to record by providing one and having them record a second. For students who are reading two or more grade levels below their current grade level, you might consider providing them with most of the information and having them read and record just one additional fact.

Accelerated students may require little direction once they have been shown how to complete a graphic organizer, and your expectations for their work may be increased. For example, if most of the class has a graphic organizer to find six facts to record, accelerated students might have a graphic organizer to find eight facts to record. Or, if most of the class is to find three commonalities between two ideas, accelerated students might be expected to find five.

Adding Technology

Graphic organizers are easily found by conducting an online search. See **Figure 5.1** for a list of online and published resources for graphic organizers

ONLINE	BOOKS
Freeology.com **www.freeology.com/graphicorgs**	*A Guide to Graphic Organizers* by James Bellanca
Houghton Mifflin Harcourt (EduPlace) **www.eduplace.com/graphicorganizer**	*The Teacher's Big Book of Graphic Organizers* by Katherine McKnight
EdHelper **www.edhelper.com/teachers/graphic_organizers.htm**	*Great Teaching with Graphic Organizers* by Patti Drapeau

Figure 5.1: RESOURCES FOR GRAPHIC ORGANIZERS.

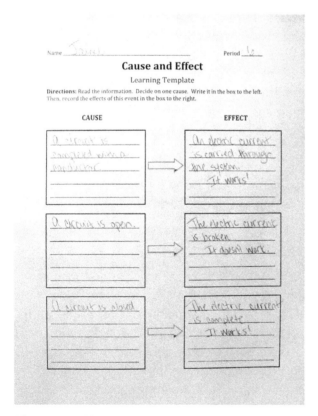

Figure 5.2: EXAMPLE OF A COMPLETED CAUSE AND EFFECT GRAPHIC ORGANIZER ON THE TOPIC OF CIRCUITS.

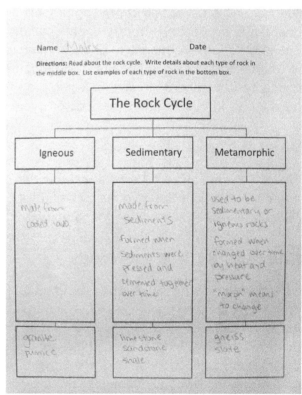

Figure 5.3: EXAMPLE OF A COMPLETED TREE DIAGRAM EXPLAINING THE THREE TYPES OF ROCKS.

Strategy 2: Writing to Preview Text

Integrated English Language Arts Skills: Previewing and Predicting; Main Idea and Details; Vocabulary Development

Description: The structure of non-fiction text is noticeably different from narrative text. Using this book as an example, it starts with a Table of Contents and is organized by chapters. Each chapter has a topic and includes headings and subheadings. Each paragraph has a main idea and supporting details. Examples by way of photos, diagrams, or charts provide visual models of the text. Important words are **bold** or *italicized*. You can find information on a particular topic quickly using the Index. If something needs clarification, it might be included in a call-out or caption off to the side.

Compare this with of the majority of fictional literature. Longer books might be broken up into chapters, but they may not have a Table of Contents to guide the reader to a particular place in the story. A novel might include pictures, but they are the illustrator's interpretation of the author's text, not examples or models to follow.

Generally, when you read a piece of fiction, you must start at the beginning and work your way through to the end. Not so with non-fiction publications. This book, for example, is not necessarily a cover-to-cover read. Some readers might choose to read it this way, but for most of us, we use the information that is most important to us personally.

Text structures like these must be brought to the forefront of students' minds when they prepare to read scientific texts. While students in primary grades might begin a new story with a picture walk or a word walk (a previewing strategy for narratives in which the teacher guides the students through the literature looking for clues as to the story's contents), intermediate students should likewise be introduced to non-fiction text by previewing and predicting. Fortunately, authors drop a lot of clues about the contents of a particular text with chapter titles, headings, subheadings, captions, diagrams, font styles, and perhaps introductory objectives and end-of-chapter questions. The Previewing Text template draws students' attention to these features and prepares them for the information they are about to receive.

Directions:

1. Provide a copy of the Previewing Text template on p. 49 for each student or pair of students.

2. List the page numbers on the board listing the students' reading assignment, or provide a copy of the informational reading selection to each student.

3. Allow students time to preview the text and complete their graphic organizers.

4. Review the organizer as a class. Discuss the information the students will read about.

TEACHER TIP

This strategy focuses students' attention on headings, subheadings, and captions. If desired, instruct students to preview the Table of Contents; highlighted, bolded, or italicized words; illustrations, charts, and photos; or other text structures unique to the reading selection.

What It Looks Like

The completed graphic organizer In **Figure 5.4** shows how a student might preview an online article. The article, "Malaria Is Still a Problem in Africa" written by Catherine Clarke Fox, was posted on the National Geographic Kids website, **www.kids.nationalgeographic.com/kids.**

The title of this text is *"Malaria Is Still a Problem in Africa"*

HEADINGS, SUBHEADINGS, CAPTIONS	KEY WORDS AND PHRASES	WHAT I THINK I WILL LEARN *OR* WHAT I ALREADY KNOW
"Mama Berta adjusts a mosquito net over her grandchild's bed."	*mosquito net*	*How mosquito nets help protect people from mosquito bites.* *I guess malaria is caused by mosquito bites.*
There were no other headings besides the title.	*malaria, Africa*	*The author will explain why malaria is a problem for people who live in Africa.* *I know that malaria is a bad disease.*
Fast Facts	*none*	*More facts about malaria.*

I think this text is about *what malaria is, and why malaria is still a problem in Africa.*

Figure 5.4: EXAMPLE OF A GRAPHIC ORGANIZER USED TO PREVIEW TEXT.

Adapting to Student Needs

Before copying the template, list the headings and subheadings in the first column of the handout for at-risk and ELL students. Allow them to work with a partner to complete the organizer. Encourage them to discuss the pictures, illustrations, diagrams, and other visuals on the page.

Accelerated students can generate questions they hope to have answered about the topic in addition to their predictions. Post these questions on a chart to refer to at the end of the lesson. In the example above, students might wonder, *"Why doesn't malaria exist in North America?"* or *"Are there other organizations besides 'Malaria No More' that help families fight malaria?"*

Adding Technology

Have students work in small groups to conduct online research about a particular topic before reading about it. Have them summarize their findings in one or two paragraphs or share downloaded images in a PowerPoint presentation with the class.

Alternatively, students can use an online photo gallery like Flickr (**www.flickr.com**) to find and share photos electronically.

Previewing Text

Directions: You are about to read about a new science topic. Before you do, use this graphic organizer to preview and predict the purpose of this text.

The title of this text is _____ .

HEADINGS, SUBHEADINGS, CAPTIONS	KEY WORDS AND PHRASES	WHAT I THINK I WILL LEARN OR WHAT I ALREADY KNOW

I think this text is about _____

Strategy 3: Making Personal Connections

Integrated English Language Arts Skills: Meta-cognition

Description: Good readers think about what they are reading as they are reading it. Just now, you are reflecting on your personal reading experiences and what you think about when reading. Now you are thinking about thinking about reading. Your schema, or background knowledge, comes into play every time you read words on a page, listen to a news report, watch a television show, or strike up a conversation with a coworker. Students, too, have some schema when they enter a science classroom. Some schemata may be limited, and some may be advanced. Regardless of students' background knowledge related to a particular topic, teachers can do much to help students make personal connections to what they learn, specifically while they are reading for information. Without the connections, no learning takes place.

Debbie Miller (2002) identifies three ways students can connect to text. She calls them "text-to-text," "text-to-self," and "text-to-world" connections (see **Figure 5.5**). The ideas in this section refer to the connections by these names. Students need to make connections to the concepts or ideas presented as well as to the text if they are to understand the content. So, although students may be engaged in a hands-on activity, they must make personal connections to the activity to make sense of it and learn from it. It's not really a "text-to-self" connection (more like an "activity-to-self" connection), but the idea is the same.

DEBBIE MILLER'S CONNECTIONS	
Text-to-Text:	Making connections between two or more texts
Text-to-Self:	Making connections between the text and one's self (experiences, ideas, memories, etc.)
Text-to-World:	Making connections between the text and events (past or present) around us that may or may not directly affect us

Figure 5.5: DEFINITIONS OF TEXT CONNECTIONS

Directions:

1. Model text-to-self, text-to-text, and text-to-world connections you make when you read a selected informational passage aloud to students.

2. Project the Making Connections template from p. 52 onto a screen and record your thoughts and ideas as they relate to the text so students can share your thinking process. The top space is for recording text-to-self connections; the middle space is for recording text-to-text connections; and the bottom space is for recording text-to-world connections.

3. Once you have provided adequate models for students to follow, provide them with a copy of the template. There are two places to record each connection.

4. Allow students the opportunity to pair-share their connections.

5. Once students become proficient in recording all three types of connections, they can begin to write freely about their connections in their science notebooks.

What It Looks Like

Figure 5.6 shows how a student might respond in her science notebook , connecting information she has read about heredity to her own personal experiences with her pet.

> Reading about DNA and genes made me think about my dog's puppies. We did not know who the father was. Six came out looking just like my dog. She has long, brown fur with a white tummy. These puppies had brown fur, and a white spot somewhere on their chests or bellies. But one puppy was jet black with no white markings. I read that genes are carried onto their offspring by the parents, so I suppose the daddy dog was black. I don't think my dog has any black fur in her genes.

Figure 5.6: SCIENCE NOTEBOOK ENTRY, "MAKING CONNECTIONS."

Adapting to Student Needs

Rather than provide at-risk and ELL students with one template to record all three types of connections, revise the assignment to have them record just one type of connection, perhaps starting with text-to-self connections. Then, as students become more comfortable thinking about their reading, encourage them to make additional connections, such as text-to-text and text-to-world.

Have accelerated students generate a list of text-to-world related issues about a particular reading assignment. Allow them time to share the connections they have considered, and justify how they stand regarding these issues. For example, students reading about heredity might discuss the issue of cloning – explaining what this is, and justifying their position on either side of the topic.

Adding Technology

- Is a picture worth a thousand words? Students may write a little more than they otherwise would if they take a digital photo of a personal connection to include in their science notebook along with their summary.

  Students can complete this task online by using the online photo gallery tool Flickr (**Flickr.com**). Alternatively, they can upload and edit their photos using Lunapic (**www.lunapic.com/editor**).

- Have students find and share online news articles connected to a real-world issue about a current science topic. Discuss how the media portray this particular issue: who the main decision or policy makers are, and how this issue affects the world around us. In other words, why is it important to know about this?

Making Connections

Directions: Making personal connections during reading can help you learn more about a topic. As you read, think about what you already know or what this information makes you think about. Record your ideas here. If there are no page numbers, leave this section blank.

PAGE(S)	PERSONAL CONNECTIONS
	As I read, I am reminded of . . .
	As I read, I remember reading or learning about . . .
	As I read, I think about the world around me. For example . . .

PAGE(S)	PERSONAL CONNECTIONS
	As I read, I am reminded of . . .
	As I read, I remember reading or learning about . . .
	As I read, I think about the world around me. For example . . .

Strategy 4: Recording on Sticky Notes

Integrated English Language Arts Skills: Main Idea and Details

Description: Sticky notes are perfect for those little memorable learning moments you want your students to capture while they are reading about a particular topic. They are small, relatively inexpensive, and extremely portable. You can take them outside for students to write on during a nature study. You can even have students jot something down while they are walking down the hallway! Sticky notes are very versatile, and they serve many purposes when students are engaged in learning.

Directions:

1. Think of a statement or question that students should answer while they are reading. Write it on a chart.

2. Provide each student with one or two sticky notes.

3. As they read, students should write information related to the statement or question on their notes.

4. Have students share their ideas with the class, and then post their note to the chart.

What It Looks Like

Figures 5.7 through **5.10** show many uses for sticky notes during science instruction.

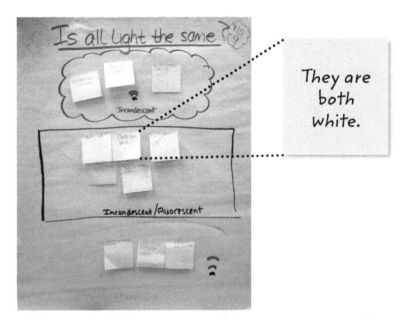

Figure 5.7: Sticky note postings: "Is all light the same?"

Figure 5.8: Sticky note postings: "What are rocks?" "How are rocks formed?" "How are rocks changed?"

Adapting to Student Needs

Allow time for at-risk and ELL students to discuss their idea(s) with a partner before committing thoughts to paper. These students could also draw and label their ideas instead of writing entire sentences.

Have accelerated students create poster summaries or PowerPoint presentations to further explain each concept. They should include a definition and example, explain why this concept is important to understand, and include one or two current events related to this topic.

Adding Technology

Instead of posting sticky notes on a chart, have students tweet or text you their ideas. The next day, share the tweets and texts with the class.

TEACHER TIP

Many companies distribute promotional sticky note pads for free, as evidenced in Figure 5.10. If you have a classroom newsletter, ask parents to send in any free pads they may have acquired. This will help reduce the cost of this consumable resource.

WHAT'S A TWEET?

A tweet is a short message (140 characters or less) posted to Twitter, an online micro-blogging service: www.twitter.com.

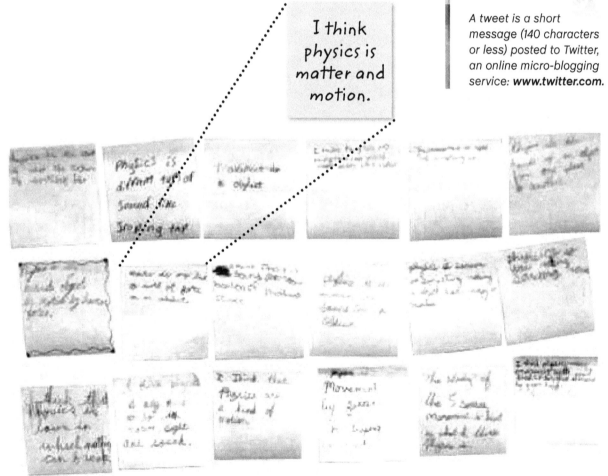

Figure 5.9: Sticky note postings: "What is physics?"

Figure 5.10: STICKY NOTE POSTINGS: "WHY IS WATER VAPOR SO IMPORTANT TO LIFE ON EARTH?"

CHAPTER SIX

Writing During Learning: *Explain—*
Listening and Thinking in Science

There are many more ways to learn about science concepts than by reading about them in textbooks, news articles, periodicals, or online informational sites. Students may also learn new information from videos, demonstrations, guest speakers, field trips, etc. Any of the previously mentioned reading strategies (see Chapter 5) work in listening situations as well. However, we as teachers like to have more than one trick up our sleeves when supporting student learning. So, here are a few additional strategies you can use when students are listening to and thinking about science.

Strategy 1: Taking Video Notes

Integrated English Language Arts Skills: Main Idea and Details

Summary: Technology has come so far! Teachers and students have ready access to a slew of marvelous, appropriate, and interesting videos and audio-visual learning segments from a host of reputable online resources. There are too many to mention, and I am sure you have your favorites. If you have not had the time to investigate for yourself, the websites in **Figure 6.1** provide quick access to videos that complement most units.

Teacher's Domain (Digital media for the classroom)
www.teachersdomain.org

National Geographic Video Collection (National Geographic video archives)
www.video.nationalgeographic.com

Newton's Apple (Over 300 video clips about science)
www.newtonsapple.tv

Figure 6.1: ONLINE RESOURCES WHERE YOU CAN FIND VIDEOS ON ALMOST EVERY SCIENCE TOPIC.

While students are watching and listening, it's the teacher's job to hold students accountable for the information they were to have gleaned from the video. This can be accomplished by a simple writing task, such as having students summarize the information on a note card, which the teacher collects and reviews to ensure adequate learning has taken place. Students can also take "free notes" in their science notebooks, but without having practiced this particular skill, students tend to write nothing or everything.

Depending on their age, grade level, intellectual ability, and prior practice, they may not have the mental aquity to listen, differentiate important ideas from non-important ideas, and synthesize these ideas in a written summary, all while the video is in continuous play. Surely, we want to lead students to this outcome. To help get them there, providing graphic organizers to complete, such as the Note Taking graphic organizer on p. 60, helps students stay focused on the main ideas of the audio-visual learning tool and supports their thinking while the video plays.

In addition to summary cards and graphic organizers, teachers can also use the sticky note idea (see p. 53), or have students generate questions about the video. Whatever the strategy used, be sure to follow up the watching-and-listening activity with some effective learning strategy, such as the ones explained here or listed below.

Directions:

Choose from among the following writing-while-watching-and-listening strategies:

- Summarize the main idea of the video on a note card.

- Record important points in science notebooks.

- Complete a ready-made graphic organizer. (See the sidebar on p. 46 for a list of graphic organizer resources.)

- Complete a video-specific graphic organizer.

- Conduct a class summary following the video. Have students record their ideas each on their own sticky note to post to a chart.

- Have students write questions they still have about the information from the video.

- Have students write quiz questions from the information presented in the video. Put students into groups of four or five and have them quiz each other using the notes they took.

What It Looks Like

Figure 6.2 shows how a student might record the steps to monitoring water quality while listening to a guest speaker from a nature preserve explain why monitoring water quality is important.

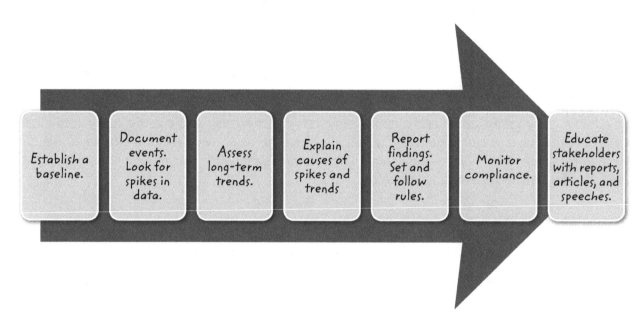

Figure 6.2: LISTENING NOTES RECORDED ON A SEQUENCE-OF-EVENTS GRAPHIC ORGANIZER.

The example in **Figure 6.3** was completed while watching a video titled, "Desert Biome" from Teacher's Domain (**www.teachersdomain.org**). The plants and animals mentioned in the video were listed to the left side of a two-column graphic organizer the teacher created specifically for this video. Students were asked to record adaptations in the right column that enabled each species to thrive in the desert climate.

PLANT OR ANIMAL	ADAPTATION(S)
Saguaro Cactus	It has the ability to store a year's worth of water.
Birds	Least adapted
Gila Woodpecker	It can peck into cactuses to make a home inside. It has food, water, and shelter there.
Lizards	It has keen eyesight. It has no pores, so it doesn't sweat.
Desert Iguana	It hunts midday. It can stand very high daytime desert temperatures.
Gambles Quail	It moves quickly. It can take water from baby cactuses.
Antelope Ground Squirrel	Can drink salty water. It has a high salt tolerance. Rarely needs to drink. Forages for seeds at midday.
Sidewinder Rattlesnake	It tests the air for food with its tongue. It hunts at night (nocturnal).
Scorpions	Nocturnal
Owls	Nocturnal

Which plants or animals above do you think would be best able to live in Florida? Why?

I think the owls could live in Florida because there is plenty of water, food, and shelter.

Figure 6.3: VIDEO NOTES

Adapting to Student Needs

Preview the video ahead of time. Write the main ideas along the left column for at-risk and ELL students. If additional scaffolding is needed, include one or two details for each main idea and instruct these students to listen for the third detail to write on the line. Over time, scale back the scaffolding until students can complete this template without any assistance.

Accelerated students can research scientists who study and investigate matters related to this topic. Allow them time to share the results of their research with the class, including photos of scientists at work.

Adding Technology

As a summative assignment, have students work in small groups to write a script for their own documentary (video) about this topic. Use video recording equipment, such as a digital camera, video camera, or computer with webcam and movie-editing software (i.e., Apple's iMovie or Windows Live Movie Maker) to record and publish student work.

Note Taking

Directions: Listen to information about a topic. While you listen, record the main ideas or key points on the left side of the paper. Pair these key points with supporting information, which you list on the right side of the paper. Use another piece of paper to summarize the information.

THESE ARE THE MAIN POINTS.	THIS INFORMATION SUPPORTS THE MAIN POINTS.
1.	1. 2. 3.
2.	1. 2. 3.
3.	1. 2. 3.

This is what I learned about _____ (topic) today.

Strategy 2: What Does This Mean to Me?

Integrated English Language Arts Skills: Drawing Conclusions; Personal Connections

Summary: Besides notetaking, another way to keep students accountable for the information they learn from a video or guest speaker is to have them reflect and respond to the information from a personal perspective. This is similar to having students make text-to-self connections (see p. 50), but the students use other media from which to make connections.

Directions:

1. Provide each student with a copy of the My View template on p. 63.

2. Have students reflect on the main points of the information.

3. Ask students to complete the organizer independently.

4. Pair the students and have them share their thoughts.

5. Discuss how the students made personal connections to the information as a class.

What It Looks Like

The science notebook entry in **Figure 6.4** was written following a presentation by an ecology expert at a local nature park. This student copied the "thinking stems" from the graphic organizer into her notebook. For a sample list of thinking stems, see p. 3.

My Thoughts

This reminded me of our water tests in class when we tested the Ph levels.

This information made me feel proud that people care about our water!

While I listened, **I imagined** all the scientists collecting water samples and analyzing them, like on CSI.

Figure 6.4: A STUDENT'S PERSONAL RESPONSE IN A SCIENCE NOTEBOOK ENTRY FOLLOWING A PRESENTATION FROM A GUEST SPEAKER. THE THINKING STEMS ARE IN BOLD TEXT.

Adapting to Student Needs

Instead of writing, then sharing, have at-risk and ELL students share, then write. You might pull them together in a small group to discuss how the information related to them, and support their writing efforts by being available to answer questions, spell unknown words, or generate additional ideas to write. Additionally, these students could be allowed to first draw their thoughts, and then use their illustrations as the starting point for their written ideas.

Accelerated students can make connections to other disciplines, such as math and social studies, or perhaps even band, art, or foreign languages. In the example from **Figure 6.4**, students might reference geographical areas that benefit from the work the visiting scientist does, or elaborate on the pH test investigation to include how they quantified their data.

Adding Technology

Find additional online videos that share similar information. Have students compare the information from both sources. They might listen for similarities or differences, or for additional examples not included in the first video.

My View

Directions: Listen to information about a topic. Think about how the information relates to you and the world around you. Record your thoughts and ideas here.

This information was about:

_____

_____

It is from (source):

_____

_____

What was the information mostly about?

_____

_____

As you listened, what did this remind you of?

_____

_____

As you listened, how did the information make you feel? Why?

_____

_____

As you listened, what did you imagine?

_____

_____

What is going on in the world around you that makes this information important?

_____

_____

What surprising or interesting information did you learn while listening?

_____

_____

If an alien visitor asked you about the information, what would you tell him?

_____

_____

_____

CHAPTER SEVEN

Writing During Learning:
Elaborate or *Extend* Learning

The fourth stage of a 5E lesson is to have students *elaborate* or *extend* their learning. Up to this point, they have thought about, messed with, and read about a particular science topic. Now it is time for students to apply and extend their learning or to learn additional information related to the topic. The elaboration stage allows additional time for students to explore ideas, processes, concepts, and skills to further the learning experience. This is also an opportunity for students to correct any lingering misconceptions they have about the topic.

Examples of elaboration activities include playing or creating board or trivia games, participating in or following case studies, conducting related experiments, or linking content to real-world application. As with any other stage of the learning process, students need time to process new and related information, record their personal thoughts and ideas, and make meaningful connections to the content. All of this can be accomplished by having students write about their learning experiences. The following pages provide simple and effective elaboration ideas that require students to demonstrate their learning through writing.

Strategy 1: Writing to Complete Projects, Problems, and Prompts

One strategy to get students to elaborate on their learning is to assign them a project, problem, or writing prompt. These can all be completed independently, or in pairs or small groups. Essentially, students must complete a task related to what they have been studying.

Projects might include research reports (see pp. 64-68), additional hands-on activities or investigations, or the construction of a three-dimentional model. All of these elaboration ideas should hold students accountable by requiring some written component in addition to the project itself. For example, if students build a three-dimentional model of a system, they should also be required to write a summary to explain how this model represents the system or object.

Problems set students to the task of resolving some conflict. Science, Technology, Engineering, and Mathematics (STEM) activities (see pp. 69-71) are perfect for this purpose.

Prompts sound boring, but they do not have to be. Consider this writing prompt:

> *You work with a team of scientists who predict that an object from space may fly too close to Earth's gravitational pull. Use what you know about the universe to devise a plan to save Earth! You must use these words: revolution, rotation, staellite, asteroid, comet, meteor, and galaxy.*

With this example, students must use what they learned about objects in space to make up some wild plan to save Earth from impending doom. Instead of a simple plan, students could write a script for a movie, including characters, setting, and dialogue. You as the science teacher can truly assess their learning by having them address a prompt this way. Students get to put all their language arts training into practice, and everyone is entertained by whatever crazy concepts they dream up.

Regardless of the project, problem, or prompt assigned to students, hold them accountable for their task by providing them with a copy of the **Project or Problem Rating Scale** (p. 82) or **Prompt Rubric** (p. 83). Be sure that students are aware of how their work will be evaluated *before* they begin working.

Strategy 2: Outside Writing Investigations and Research Projects

Integrated English Language Arts Skills: Planning; Researching; Summarizing

Description: Classroom time restraints may require elaboration activities to be assigned as homework or outside class time. Or, for extensive research projects, students might spend some class time completing their work while some of the work is completed outside of class. One way to research more in a short amount of time is to divide and conquer. Assign each small group of students one smaller component of a larger research project. The goups can them combine their findings into one complete project.

Be aware that research projects tend to engage students in the low-level skills of knowledge and comprehension. We like to think that we are requiring students to synthesize information, a high-level skill, but this is not the case. Synthesis requires original thought in a novel and unique situation. Regurgitating facts and information from others' published work is simply a summarizing task. Compare this with a science fair summary. When students write their report, they must start with only the information they gathered through experimentation. There is a research (background information) component, but most of the report is derived from data and includes an explanation of the findings. This work is completely synthesized by the student.

To elevate the cognitive level of a typical research project, you might consider requiring students to include a statement or two explaining why this information is important to know, or how these facts apply to their community. Another idea is to have students write the report from the perspective of a scientist involved in this field. Or, you could have students change their report into a persuasive essay.

Directions:

1. Have students select a topic to research. Provide suggestions for appropriate and interesting topics, if needed.

2. Make one copy of the Research Project activity sheet on p. 68 for each student.

3. Provide guidelines for conducting research. Inform students of specific criteria, such as how many references to cite or include, the format you prefer (typed or handwritten), and whether they should include pictures, illustrations, or diagrams.

4. Specific criteria such as those listed in step three will affect the evaluation rubric you use to assess student work. Make the necessary adjustments to the rubric. You can modify the **Research Report Rubric** on p. 84 or make your own.

5. Give students a copy of the evaluation rubric. Review it with them. Be sure they understand how their work will be evaluated.

6. If possible, reserve class time for students to conduct their research, organize their ideas, and write their first draft. Conference with students regarding their progress and consider establishing completion goals with the class (i.e., research completed by a certain date, first draft completed by a certain date, etc.). Be sure students are aware of the deadline for completion and of the consequences for submitting late work.

What It Looks Like

If students can dream it, it can happen! Reports come in all shapes and sizes, from murals to posters to typed or handwritten reports. As students begin to develop their research project ideas, help them pick the best medium through which to publish their work. Some reports are best presented as a typed document while others are better off using video recording equipment (such as if students conducted an interview with a famous scientist.) If you're not choosey about the format of the project, allow students the freedom to imagine and develop their own ideas. If you would rather everyone submit a typed report, make your expectations clear before students begin researching.

Adapting to Student Needs

On a daily basis, make time for conferencing with at-risk and ELL students regarding their project progress. Support their efforts by suggesting or finding text resources at suitable reading levels. You might also provide additional graphic organizers for them to complete to help them organize their ideas.

Accelerated students can complete alternatives to traditional reports by organizing their summary in any one of the following formats:

- ABC book (a composite of pages with each page highlighting a key term that begins with each subsequent letter of the alphabet: atom, bromide, carbon, etc.)

- An article for a scientific journal or newspaper

- Diary entries from the perspective of a scientist in this field

- Interview with a scientist in this field

- Radio report

- Scrapbook

- Technical manual

- Webpage

Adding Technology

- Require students to use the World Wide Web to conduct at least some of their research. This is also an opportune moment in your students' education to discuss which websites are best for research purposes, and which are not. Conduct a lesson on finding and using reliable Internet resources, or ask your school or district's technology department for assistance. Show students how to cite these types of resources (in addition to text resources) appropriately.

- Allow students to make a podcast or an edited video about their project. Visit PoducateMe.com (**www.poducateme.com/guide**) for a free, step-by-step guide to podcasting. For an overview of the free audio editing software Audacity, visit **www.manual.audacityteam.org** and click through the "Tutorials" section. If you'd like to see some examples of podcasts created by (and for) educators, visit the Education Podcast Network: **www.epnweb.org**.

Research Project

Topic: _____

_____

Purpose for Writing: Why are you writing this paper? _____

_____

_____

Conduct your research.   Use other paper or note cards. Write down facts and information you believe is important. Be sure to reference your facts. You should be able to find the information quickly if asked.

Organize your ideas.   Group the information you found. Decide on the main ideas. Then, list the details that support each main idea.

MAIN IDEA 1	MAIN IDEA 2	MAIN IDEA 3
DETAILS	**DETAILS**	**DETAILS**

Write your first draft.   Use notebook paper or a word processing program. Write freely. Do not be concerned about grammar, punctuation, or spelling just yet. Write to get all the information down on the page.

Review your work.   Re-read your whole report. Make sure you included all the important information. Make revisions, as needed.

Edit your work.   Now you can check spelling, grammar, and punctuation. Each paragraph should be indented. Fix what you need to fix.

Write your final draft. This is your final product. It should be neat, organized, and include all essential information. This one counts! Take pride in your work.

Strategy 3: Science, Technology, Engineering, and Mathematics (STEM) Activities: Writing for Science in the Real World

STEM activities are perfect problem-solving tasks for students. They set up a situation, pose a challenge of some sort, and require students to devise a plan to resolve the conflict. For example, when studying space travel, students might be presented with the problem of prioritizing what to bring on a colonization mission, knowing they can only bring five things.

They might be asked to design and construct a prototype for a bird feeder suitable for birds, but not for pesky squirrels who like to steal all the bird food. They might be presented the challenge of designing and creating a prototype for an alert system for dangerous weather in their area that serves their entire community. To embed writing as a critical element to these types of activities, students can record their ideas, plan their prototype, and summarize their results.

Directions

1. Write the task students are to accomplish on the lines at the top of the STEM learning template p. 71.

2. Make one copy of the activity sheet for each small group of students.

3. Have each group assign one person as the recorder.

4. Provide the needed materials, space, and time for students to complete their prototype.

5. Reserve class time for students to share their prototypes and evaluate their effectiveness.

6. Use the **Project or Problem Rating Scale** on p. 82 to evaluate student work.

What It Looks Like

Figure 7.1 is an example of a STEM project related to a system to defy gravity. Students studied the effects of gravity and were challenged to design and create a system that would allow a ball to move in a continuous circle with no outside forces acting on it. Following this activity, they read about centripetal force and watched videos of people trying to rollerskate in a circle without outside forces.

> **Challenges of rolling a ball in a circle:** We could not get the ball to roll in a circle without an outside force. We tried spinning it when we rolled it because a bowling ball will curve sometimes when you do this. This didn't work, either. Maybe there is not enough friction between the floor and the ball.
>
> **Our plan:** We will try tying a string to the ball and swinging it around. We will also build a foil track for the ball, and see if it will move in a circle following the track.

Figure 7.1: STUDENTS' RECORD KEEPING IN A STEM ACTIVITY.

Adapting to Student Needs

Be sure at-risk and ELL students are paired with students who can write for the group. Encourage collaboration among all the group members. Instruct students to hear from everyone in the group before they decide on one particular prototype. At various stages of completion, ask these students to summarize what is happening in the group. This will ensure involvement from everyone, including those who may not be successful with written tasks.

Challenge accelerated students to create an advertisement for their prototype. They can write a script that includes everyone in their group, and organize the selection of props and actions by the "actors."

Adding Technology

Share electronic photos, diagrams, and videos of real-life prototypes related to this activity. Project them on a screen, and have students discuss the value of the items' uses in society. Also discuss the math and science that people involved in the project will likely need to know to accomplish their goal.

STEM

Task: _____

_____

Identify the problem. What do you need to do? _____

_____

Make a plan. How will you attempt to resolve this problem? _____

_____

_____

_____

As part of your plan, sketch what the prototype will look like on another sheet of paper. Label its parts.

Design and construct your prototype. What challenges did you face? _____

_____

_____

Test your prototype. If you collect data, record it on another sheet of paper.

Was your prototype successful? Why or why not? _____

_____

_____

Evaluate your prototype. Will you make modifications to the design? Why or why not? What modifications will you make? _____

_____

_____

Communicate your results. Share your experience with your class.

CHAPTER EIGHT

Writing Strategies to *Evaluate* Student Learning

Finally. A science unit has come to a close. Students have touched, prodded, analyzed, comprehended, considered, evaluated, compared, connected, and synthesized information. Now we have to have a way to evaluate their learning and quantify it in some way for a grade.

There are many theories on evaluating and grading student work. You likely have your system in place, and are quite satisfied with it. But does it truly reflect the level of understanding students can demonstrate for a particular topic, and the concepts, content, and skills contained within it? If grading and evaluating student work is a topic of interest to you, and you want to learn more about it, you might consider reading any of these three resources:

- *Ahead of the Curve: The Power of Assessment to Transform Teaching and Learning.* Edited by Douglas Reeves. Published by Solution Tree, 2007.

- *Classroom Assessment & Grading That Work.* Written by Robert J. Marzano. Published by the Association for Supervision and Curriculum Development (ASCD), 2006.

- *Educative Assessment: Designing Assessments to Inform and Improve Student Performance.* Written by Grant Wiggins. Published by Jossey-Bass, 1998.

The ideas in this book have not addressed any particular science topic (*what* students should know), but they do provide strategies for supporting student learning (*how* students learn) through the 5E method. This chapter explores ideas and suggestions for determing whether students reached a disirable outcome (whether they "got it"). Regardless of your process for grading, the ideas in this chapter provide strategies for determining students' levels of understanding through writing.

Strategy 1: Writing for the Purpose of Formative Assessment

Hopefully, teachers do not wait until the end of a unit to discover whether students have learned the information, processes, and skills required by their standards and benchmarks. By then, it is too late. Formative assessments occur throughout the learning process, starting with an informal assessment of student misconceptions and prior knowledge before teaching even begins. This allows teachers to adjust the teaching process, thereby allowing students who need additional instruction to truly learn a particular topic or concept to have the time they need. These suggestions will help teachers determine whether students are on track meet the objectives of the unit before a summative, end-of-unit assessment occurs.

Notebook Review	This book started with an overview of the use of notebooks throughout a unit of study (see Chapter 1). As students record and respond in their notebooks, teachers can easily monitor students' understanding and thinking by simply walking around as students write, checking a notebook here or there, or by collecting notebooks for review weekly. Not every notebook needs a review every day or on one certain day. Break up the task by monitoring or collecting just five or six notebooks each day. By the end of the week, every student will have had his record-keeping checked.
Exit Cards	If checking notebooks is not feasible, have students respond to the information presented on exit cards once weekly. This is a simple strategy that allows a teacher to guage his or her students' levels of understanding of a particular topic with minimal resources, and it takes just five minutes at the end of class one day. Distribute a note card to each student, preferably one that is blank on one side and lined on the other. Pose a question or simple task to students such as "Explain the Coriolis effect" or "If you were a protist, what would you be, and why?" Students can use the blank side of the card to illustrate their ideas, then use the lined side to write to explain. The cards do not allow for a lot of writing, so checking for formative purposes may be accomplished in a short amount of time.
One-sentence Summary	Another option to exit cards is to have students write a one-sentence summary on a strip of notebook paper. A question as simple as, "What did you learn today?" will provide the teacher with insights regarding his or her students' initial understandings. A one-sentence summary sounds very simple. However, this can pose quite a challenge for students. Before setting students to this task, provide one or two examples on the board or allow students to think aloud with a neighbor before putting pencil to paper.

Engage, Explore, Explain

Chapters 2-6 shared ideas to help students learn through writing during the *engage*, *explore*, and *explain* stages of a 5E science lesson. With every step came some opportunity for students to demonstrate their understanding through writing. Teachers can use student work as a means to assess whether they are grasping the ideas presented in the unit of study as it progresses. For example, did the student recording information from the video on p. 59 really "get" adaptations? His response at the bottom of the organizer that "owls could live in Florida because there is plenty of water, food, and shelter" does not really demonstrate his understanding of adaptations. Every animal needs food, water, and shelter. A better question might have been, "Which animal from the list is least adapted to live in Florida and why?" Additionally, students were asked to list three reasons why cactuses are adapted to live in a desert environment. Following an activity for each stage of the lesson (engage, explore, and explain) students should easily have been able to respond to this question. A simple response on an exit card or in their science notebooks provided the teacher with additional information regarding whether students truly understood this idea or not.

Quiz Me

Students do not necessarily need to complete a long, formal test to demonstrate their learning during a unit of study. Instead, short, deliberate quizzes may provide teachers adequate feedback related to where students are in the learning process. Multiple-choice quizzes are one option, but they generally do not encompass a wide-enough range of concepts, nor are they long enough for students to truly demonstrate what they know and don't know. Additionally, one never really knows if students are guessing, or if they really do know the answer. Instead, consider using any of the writing activities from any chapter in this book to determine how far students have come with regard to their learning. For example, you might post a list of related terms, and have students group them on a sheet of paper and justify their categories (See Figure 4.6). A quick check will inform the teacher whether students have really learned the words, or whether they remain a little lost. Or, have students complete a main idea and detail or compare/contrast graphic organizer using their notes about a particular topic (See Chapter 5). Notes are supposed to provide students with a reflection of learning. If they can't accomplish this simple task given this level of support, students have not really grasped the main concepts you are trying to teach them.

If students seem off-track at any point during a lesson or unit, or if they do not respond as thoroughly as you would have hoped, take the opportunity to re-teach this particular concept. You could engage students in a pair-share activity, video, demonstration, or other simple activity to allow them additional time to explore a particular idea and revisit their understanding of the topic or concept. Alternatively, the elaborate stage of a 5E lesson is also an opportunity for students to "practice science." Provide students with additional learning opportunities to support their understandings and extend or revise their thinking through writing.

Strategy 2: Writing for the Purpose of Summative Assessment

At the end of a unit comes some form of summative assessment. This is a culminating evaluation regarding the information, topics, and concepts students learned from a comprehensive unit. End-of-chapter tests are summative assessments. State tests are summative assessments. They encompass a wide range of objectives and are usually formatted as multiple choice, matching, or fill-in-the-blank questions. These types of questions are easy to score, but they usually do not require students to do a whole lot of thinking. If a student answers C (the correct answer) to question 16, can you be sure that he understood this idea–or did he simply guess well? The strategies that follow are summative in nature, and they provide the teacher with more concrete evidence of student mastery of the content.

Tell Me Why

A simple strategy to elevate student thinking during guess-and-check tests is to have them explain off to the side *how* they knew C was the correct answer. Or, even more challenging, they can explain how they knew A, B, and D were *not* the correct answers. The teacher can choose any one or two questions for students to respond to in this fashion, or the teacher can allow students to choose their own. It is not a daunting task for students to write to explain their thinking to one or two questions, and it is not a daunting task for teachers to grade all these summaries. Using a simple scale of 0-4 is sufficient (see **Figure 8.1**).

> **4-Point Scale for Grading Written Response Questions**
> 0 – No understanding
> 1 – Minimal understanding
> 2 – Partial understanding
> 3 – Some understanding
> 4 – Thorough understanding

Figure 8.1: 4-POINT SCALE

Storyline

Another summative assessment idea is to have students write a story, poem, article, tribute, or folktale about the main topic from a unit of study, using all the related terms they encountered as part of their script. Use the **Prompt Rubric** on p. 83 to evaluate student work. Be sure they understand that the clarity of their ideas will provide the feedback you need regarding their understanding. For example, students cannot simply include characters named Sir Cumference, Gram, and Little Liter in their story. If they are writing a mystery about scientific systems of measurement, they need to have a character measure the circumference of something for a particular purpose to demonstrate their understanding of measurement and its uses in scientific investigations.

Strategy 3: Project-based Outcomes

Performance tasks, or project-based assignments, provide an alternative to traditional tests. When formatted and developed correctly, teachers can determine how well their students understood a particular science topic or concept. The benefit of performance tasks is that they allow students the freedom to be creative, reach out beyond the facts, and really demonstrate their learning through personal and individualized means. The biggest drawback to performance-based measures is that they are typically much more time consuming than tests for both students and teachers, and they require extensive planning, resources, and materials than traditional paper-pencil tests.

Additionally, some projects, such as the construction of three-dimensional models or dioramas, do not inherently lend themselves to some writing task. Teachers might be able to see, literally, how their students interpret particular details with these types of projects. However, they might not be able to accurately gauge the level of student learning. Fortunately, this dilemma is easily corrected by requiring summaries through display cards, book jackets, debates, descriptions, flip charts, memos, audio recordings, reviews, or brochures, to name a few.

When developing performance tasks, Wiggins (1998) cautions teachers to ensure their authenticity, credibility/validity, and high level of engagement. He suggests these simplified steps to developing such assessment activities (p. 147):

1. Think of or find an activity to use to assess a particular or set of objectives.

2. If this activity cannot reliably assess the objectives, modify it so that it can.

3. Determine the criteria needed to complete the activity.

4. Develop a rubric to reflect the criteria and target objectives.

5. Evaluate the design of the task. Be sure it is engages students, provides regular intervals of feedback for students, allows for an appropriate amount of latitude on the part of the student for completion, has clear directions and expectations, and will provide useful feedback for the teacher regarding students' learning.

Below are three examples of performance tasks students might complete to culminate a unit related to plant reproduction, rocks and minerals, and natural resources. The **Project or Problem Rating Scale** on p. 82 is generic but provides suggested criteria upon which to evaluate student work—and it leaves room for you to write in the specific criteria you want to see. When assigning larger projects, you may want to use the rubric provided as a guide, and include more specific criteria related to the objectives of the unit and the project as part of the overall evaluation. For example, in the first project, you might include criteria evaluating the effectiveness of the design and the level of detail related to each of the conditions for optimal plant growth.

Sample Project-Based Assessments

GOLDEN GROWTH

A local florist wants to expand her inventory of flowering plants. She seeks the help of your botany class. She wants to know the best flowering plants to grow in her area and the steps she needs to take to design and construct a structure to house them so that they have the best chance of growth. You accept her challenge.

Plan a structure to house two or more flowering plants. Identify the conditions in which the plants will grow: space, temperature, light, insect activity, soil composition, water, and germination projections. Identify the plants that will grow the best in the conditions you have established.

Draw a design for the structure. Write a detailed report outlining the steps the owner of the flower shop needs to take to maximize each condition. Explain how insect activity is a vital part of the system. Include a table or chart to show projected plant population growth for the next six months.

DIAMOND DIG

Your friend is going on a family trip. He is very excited because he believes he will find diamonds lying on the ground. You, however, are skeptical that this will happen so easily. You decide to do a little research to help out your friend.

Diamonds are a naturally occurring mineral. They formed deep underground millions of years ago. So, how did they get to the earth's surface? Conduct research to find out how diamond deposits might have developed where people can find them. Locate the most common deposit areas around the globe. Find out whether people can just find diamonds lying on the ground.

Write your friend a letter. Explain the results of your research. Explain what minerals are. Explain how they are different from rocks. Explain how they contribute to the makeup of the earth, and how a person can tell by the mineral's properties whether it is a real diamond. Describe the conditions under which most diamonds are discovered, and how miners work to extract them from the earth. Include a world map. Draw a key to show the most common places to find diamonds, and where your friend might stumble across some lying on the ground, if this information is part of your findings. If not, tell him why this is unlikely.

BEING ENERGY EFFICIENT IN A GREEN WORLD

Many people are "going green." This means they are determined to use renewable resources to build their homes and live their lives. They also want to conserve energy over a long period. The question is: do renewable resources allow people to conserve energy?

You decide to test the efficiency of some renewable and nonrenewable resources as they relate to heating and cooling. Design an experiment that will allow you to test the efficiency of two or more resources: one renewable and one nonrenewable.

Complete the planning and beginning report stages of the project. Include in your report the purpose for the project, the materials you would use to set it up, the steps you would follow to conduct the experiment, and the expected outcomes. In your purpose, include reasons to support or refute the use of renewable resources. List examples of renewable resources people might use in the construction of their homes, and how these differ from nonrenewable resources. If possible, complete the experiment. Include data tables and charts in your report, an analysis of the data collected, and a summary of the results.

CHAPTER NINE

Rubrics for Evaluating Student Work

One essential component of any unit plan includes a process, strategy, or system for determining the level of student proficiency with regard to the skills and information they were to have learned from instruction. In other words, how will you evaluate students' understanding, and how will you grade them? This idea was discussed to some extent in the previous chapter when differentiating between formative (informal) and summative (formal) assessments.

Some evaluation strategies (such as tests and quizzes) naturally lend themselves to quantifying student achievement. Each question is worth so many points, which add up to a certain percentage grade. Most writing assignments, however, are much more subjective in nature.

To this author, the most unfair practice a teacher can hold is to assign a written task to students without having considered how it will be used to evaluate student understanding or its value toward their overall grade. One approach to evaluating students' written work more objectively is to pair them with rubrics, rating scales, or checklists. Although these three evaluation techniques are similar, each serves a slightly different purpose and each provides a different level of specificity in the evaluation of student work.

Rubrics vs. Rating Scales vs. Checklists

Rubrics, rating scales, and checklists are some of the ways teachers can evaluate (or grade) student work. A rubric is very detailed. It tells students the exact elements that matter the most in their projects, and it defines the exact criteria related to the quality of the work that will be used in the evaluation. The **Research Report Rubric** on p. 84 is an example of a rubric.

A rating scale is a modified rubric. It is less specific regarding the quality of each criterion being evaluated. The **Lab Report Rating Scale** on p. 80 is an example of a rating scale. The criteria for evaluating student work mirrors what students might see in a rubric, but the scale is less specific, more subjective, and less definitive.

Checklists are simple lists of tasks to review, and they receive a yes/no response or check if completed. These are useful for students to self-evaluate their work prior to submitting it for review. The **Project Completion Checklist** on p. 86 is an example of a checklist. Some teachers assign numeric quantities to each criterion, depending on its importance, and use this score as part of the overall evaluation of the student's grade.

When assigning larger tasks that are best evaluated using rubrics or rating scales, be sure to distribute the evaluation criteria at the onset of the project. Review the criteria with the class. Be sure everyone is clear and has a record of how their work will be graded. If possible, leave room for student- and teacher-written comments regarding the work in progress, as well as the final product.

Feedback

One critical element to the completion of projects is the use of regular feedback. Susan Brookhart (2008) suggests making "as many opportunities as you can to give students positive messages about how they are doing relative to the learning targets and what might be useful to do next." (p. 59) This might be accomplished through small group feedback, whole-class feedback, or individual feedback, depending on the instructional level of students and the skill-appropriateness of the task. Assigning a project and setting a due date with no communication in between leaves students wondering, questioning, and worrying over whether they are on the right track, or whether their projects will meet with your approval. This is the part of science that most closely mirrors language arts. In language arts, students are likely learning the process of writing: brainstorming, drafting, revising, editing, and publishing. You, however, are the science teacher. Your students are learning about bugs, slugs, and sludge. Longer projects are valuable learning and assessment tools. Many students enjoy them, and teachers can have a tremendous sense of accomplishment regarding their science instruction when they see the exemplary work coming back to them from their students in this fashion. For optimal work, students need regular feedback. So, how do you provide the language arts (specifically, the writing process) support students need when you are not a writing teacher?

First, you might try collaborating with the language arts teachers. Let them know about your project ahead of time, and ask their opinion of the task. They may offer suggestions that will really elevate the interest, rigor, and relevance of the project. Then, have them review the evaluation criteria you plan to use, or ask them for a rubric they use. This is an opportunity for you to hold students accountable for what they have been learning in language arts and apply it in a science report. The language arts teachers will thank you! Hopefully, they will offer (if not, you can suggest it) to provide feedback to the students as they complete their projects. They might also have suggestions for providing time for feedback during science class that will not intrude fully on your class time.

Another option for providing regular feedback is to be available before or after school for students, or to arrange time during the school day when they might stop by to see you. If daytime is not possible, students can post their projects to a secure blog or website, or they can email it to you at different stages of completion. You can then access students' work anytime from any computer, include suggestions for changes, or post positive and encouraging comments to keep students motivated and interested.

Finally, peer review is another viable and useful option for providing regular feedback to students. When time is short, students can pair up to take on the roll of listener and observer, and offer thoughtful feedback to the students doing the sharing. Do not assume that students know how to do this. A little time spent early in the school year modeling and practicing effective feedback will save time in the long run.

You are just one person. To meet with each of twenty-five students individually in a fifty-minute period, each student has the benefit of your ear for on average just two minutes. However, if students are paired or in small groups to provide feedback, each student could have up to five minutes to share his or her progress with a partner. Once both partners have had a chance to share, only ten minutes of class time has been used for this purpose, leaving a full forty minutes to continue with instruction. Your language arts professionals may have additional suggestions for developing a classroom environment that promotes positive peer feedback. Use their skills and talents to your advantage to get the most out of your instructional time for the overall benefit of student learning.

Lab Report Rating Scale

CRITERIA	EARNED	POSSIBLE
Completeness All parts of lab are completed.	_____	20
Thoroughness All parts of lab have thorough summaries.	_____	20
Quality of Work Lab is neat and easy to read.	_____	20
Collaboration Group worked collaboratively on lab.	_____	20
Independent Contributions Student was a valuable, contributing lab member.	_____	20
TOTAL	_____	**100**

Data Analysis Rubric

	4	3	2	1
Organization	Data are well organized and clearly identified.	Data are somewhat organized and somewhat clear.	Data may lack organization or clarity.	Data are neither organized nor clear.
Chart Type	Chart type is completely appropriate for data.	Chart type is appropriate, but could be improved.	Chart type is inappropriate or incorrectly completed.	Chart type is inappropriate and completed incorrectly.
Chart Components	Chart includes axes labels, measurement labels, title, and key.	Chart includes axes labels, measurement labels, title, and key, but some information may be lacking.	Chart includes only one or two: axes labels, measurement labels, title, and key.	Chart does not include any labels, a title, or a key.
Data	Chart consistently and accurately reflects collected data.	Chart somewhat reflects collected data correctly.	Chart partially reflects collected data.	Chart does not reflect collected data.

TOTAL: _____ / 16

Project or Problem Rating Scale

Project Title: _____ Student: _____	0 Not Evident	1 Needs Work	2 Good	3 Strong	4 Outstanding	TOTAL
Project completed following directions						
Includes _____ _____ _____						
Writing is appropriate to format						
Grammar, spelling, and punctuation are correct						
Writing demonstrates understanding of science concept						
Overall impression						

TOTAL: _____ / 24

Positives:

One area to improve:

Prompt Rubric

Title _____

Name _____ Period _____

	4 Outstanding	3 Good	2 Fair	1 Needs Work
TOPIC	Writing is on topic from start to finish.	Writing is on topic, but lacks coherency.	Writing is somewhat on topic, but lapses occur.	Writing is not on topic.
CONTENT	Writing has ample details, vivid descriptions, and specific vocabulary.	Writing has some supportive details, adequate descriptions, and/or mostly specific vocabulary.	Writing has few details that may not support the main ideas, few (if any) descriptions, and some unspecific vocabulary.	Writing lacks any supportive details, descriptions, and/or specific vocabulary.
ORGANIZATION	Writing is well organized.	Writing is somewhat organized.	Writing has little organization.	Writing lacks any organization.
THOROUGHNESS	Writing is complete and thorough.	Writing is mostly complete but may not be fully thorough.	Writing is somewhat complete, but lacks thoroughness.	Writing is incomplete and not thorough.
CONVENTIONS	Writing includes correct grammar, spelling, and punctuation.	Writing includes mostly correct grammar, spelling, and punctuation.	Writing includes incorrect grammar, spelling, and punctuation.	Very little grammar, spelling, and punctuation are correct.

TOTAL: _____ / 20

Teacher Comments:

Research Report Rubric

	4 Outstanding	3 Good	2 Fair	1 Needs Work
TOPIC OR CONCEPT	Topic is relevant to a recent unit of study. It has tremendous value as a research project. The topic sentence has value to today's reader.	Topic is relevant to a recent unit of study. It has some value as a research project. The topic sentence has value to today's reader, but may be unclear.	Topic may be relevant to a recent unit of study. It has limited value as a research project. The topic sentence may have value to today's reader, but it is unclear.	Topic is irrelevant to a recent unit of study. It has little value as a research project. Topic sentence is missing or unclear.
SOURCES	Student utilized highly appropriate and reliable sources: books, journals, and electronic sources	Student utilized appropriate and reliable sources: books, journals, and electronic sources	Student utilized at least one appropriate or reliable source: book, journal, or electronic source	Student utilized inappropriate or unreliable sources: books, journals, or electronic sources
ORGANIZATION OF CONTENT	Report is well organized with a clear beginning, middle, and end.	Report is organized with a beginning, middle, and end, but some content may be misplaced.	Report may be organized with a beginning, middle, or end, but not all three.	Report is unorganized with no clear beginning, middle, or end.
DETAILS	Supporting information is clearly and directly related to each main point. The details offer substantial support of main ideas.	Supporting information is mostly clear and directly related to each main point. The details offer strong support of main ideas.	Supporting information may be unclear or indirectly related to each main point. The details offer limited support of main ideas.	Supporting information is unclear and indirectly related to each main point. The details offer little to no support of main ideas.

Title _____

Name _____ **Period** _____

	4 Outstanding	3 Good	2 Fair	1 Needs Work
VOCABULARY	Report uses substantial, highly specific scientific vocabulary.	Report uses adequate, specific scientific vocabulary.	Report uses some specific, scientific vocabulary.	Report uses little to no specific, scientific vocabulary.
ANCILLARIES	Report includes adequate charts, diagrams, photos, illustrations, or other supporting features directly related to the text.	Report includes charts, diagrams, photos, illustrations, or other supporting features related to the text, but some may be unclear.	Report includes at least one chart, diagram, photo, illustration, or other supporting feature related to the text.	Report has no charts, diagrams, photos, illustrations, or other supporting features related to the text.
OVERALL REVIEW	Report is complete and thorough. It is written neatly with mostly correct grammar, punctuation, and spelling.	Report is complete but not fully thorough. It is generally neat with mostly correct grammar, punctuation, and spelling.	Report is incomplete or not fully thorough. It lacks neatness and has some incorrect grammar, punctuation, and spelling.	Report is incomplete and not thorough. It lacks neatness and has incorrect grammar, punctuation, and spelling.

TOTAL: _____ / 28

Teacher Comments:

Project Completion Checklist

Directions: Review the directions for the scientific investigation or project. Use this checklist as a self-evaluation to determine whether you are ready to turn in your project.

Report Content

❑ My project has a clear beginning, middle, and end.

❑ I have something great to say. My main idea is clear. It is stated in the introduction and conclusion.

❑ My details are directly related to, and supportive of, the main idea.

❑ My project moves easily from one idea to the next. I use appropriate and varied transitions.

❑ Each paragraph has a topic sentence and supporting details.

❑ The vocabulary I use is specific and precise.

❑ I include just enough charts, diagrams, or illustrations to support the content. They are labeled with captions, and their purpose is clear.

❑ My spelling, punctuation, and grammar are correct.

Just the Facts

❑ I use facts and evidence, not opinions, when completing my work.

❑ I use two or more reliable sources to find facts and information.

❑ My list of sources is complete.

Overall

❑ My work is my own. I use my own words and stayed true to my own ideas.

❑ My project reflects my writing style.

❑ My project is interesting to read.

Something I had trouble with was: _____

_____

_____

I (circle one):   DID   DID NOT   enjoy this assignment because:

_____

_____

_____

"Apple iLife '11: iMovie," http://www.apple.com/ilife/imovie (accessed August 18, 2011).

"Audacity,"http://audacity.sourceforge.net (accessed August 18, 2011).

Bellanca, J. *A Guide to Graphic Organizers*. Thousand Oaks, CA: Corwin Press, 2007.

Brookhart, S. M. "Feedback that Fits." *Educational Leadership*. Vol. 65, No. 4, 2008.

Bybee, R. W., et.al. *The BSCS 5E Instructional Model: Origins, Effectiveness, and Applications*. Executive Summary. BSCS Colorado Springs, CO: July, 2006.

Common Core State Standards Initiative. Introduction, English Language Arts Standards. Retrieved from http://www.corestandards.org/the-standards/english-language-arts-standards, 2010.

"Discovery Kids," http://kids.discovery.com (accessed July 20, 2011).

Drapeau, P. *Great Teaching with Graphic Organizers*. New York, NY: Scholastic, Inc., 1998.

"edHelper.com," http://edhelper.com/teachers/graphic_organizers.htm (accessed July 20, 2011).

"Education Place," Houghton Mifflin Harcourt. http://www.eduplace.com/graphicorganizer (accessed July 20, 2011).

"The Education Podcast Network," http://epnweb.org (accessed August 18, 2011).

Eisenkraft, A. "Expanding the 5E Model." *The Science Teacher*. Vol. 70, No. 6, 2003.

"Flickr," http://www.flickr.com (accessed July 20, 2011).

Fox, C. "Malaria Is Still a Problem in Africa" from *National Geographic for Kids* online (kids.nationalgeographic.com/kids/stories/spacescience/malaria), 2011.

"Glogster EDU." http://edu.glogster.com (accessed July 20, 2011).

"Google Apps for Education," http://www.google.com/apps/intl/en/edu (accessed August 18, 2011).

"Google Docs Tour," Google. http://www.google.com/google-d-s/tour1.html (accessed July 20, 2011).

"Graphic Organizers," Freeology. http://freeology.com/graphicorgs (accessed July 20, 2011).

Godin, D. *Amazing Hands-on Literature Projects for Secondary Students*. Gainesville, FL: Maupin House Publishing, 2010.

Harvey, S. *Non-fiction Matters: Reading, Writing, and Research in Grades 3 – 8*. Portland, ME: Stenhouse Publishers, 1998.

Hunter, M. *Mastery Teaching*. Thousand Oaks, CA: Corwin Press, Inc, 1982.

"Intodit.com," http://www.intodit.com (accessed July 20, 2011).

Just Read Now: Frayer Model. "Just Read Now!," http://www.justreadnow.com/strategies/frayer.htm (accessed July 20, 2011).

Kidspiration and *Inspiration* software are trademarks of Inspiration Software, Inc., 9400 SW Beaverton-Hillsdale Hwy, Suite 300, Beaverton, OR, 97005. (503) 297-3004

"LunaPic Online Photo Editor," http://lunapic.com/editor (accessed July 20, 2011).

Marzano, R. *Classroom Instruction that Works.* Alexandria, VA: Association for Supervision and Curriculum Development, 2001.

Marzano, R. *Classroom Assessment and Grading that Work.* Alexandria, VA: Association for Supervision and Curriculum Development, 2006.

McGregor, T. *Comprehension Connections: Bridges to strategic reading.* Portsmouth, NH: Heinemann, 2007.

McKay, D. R. "Writing Skills: Why Writing Skills Are Important." *About.com.* Retrieved from http://careerplanning.about.com/cs/miscskills/a/writing_skills.htm, 2011.

McKnight, K. The Teacher's Big Book of Graphic Organizers: San Francisco, CA: Jossey-Bass, 2010.

Microsoft® Office products are available from http://www.microsoftstore.com.

Miller, D. *Reading with Meaning: Teaching Comprehension in the Primary Grades.* Portland, ME: Stenhouse Publishers, 2002.

National Geographic Kids Magazine is available for purchase: "National Geographic Subscriptions," National Geographic. http://www.natgeomagazines.com (accessed July 20, 2011).

"National Geographic Kids," http://kids.nationalgeographic.com/kids (accessed July 20, 2011).

"PoducateMe.com," http://poducateme.com (accessed August 18, 2011).

Reeves, D. *Ahead of the Curve: The Power of Assessment to Transform Teaching and Learning.* Bloomington, IN: Solution Tree, 2007.

Report of the National Commission on Writing in America's Schools and Colleges. *The Neglected "R": A need for a writing revolution.* The College Entrance Examination Board, April, 2003.

Report of the National Commission on Writing in America's Schools and Colleges. *Writing: A Ticket to Work... Or a Ticket Out. A Survey of Business Leaders.* The College Entrance Examination Board, September, 2004.

"Scribblar," http://www.scribblar.com (accessed July 20, 2011).

Simmons, K. and Guinn, C. *Bookbag of the Bag Ladies Best.* Gainesville, FL: Maupin House Publishing, 2000.

"Teachers' Domain," http://www.teachersdomain.org (accessed July 20, 2011).

"Tumblr," http://www.tumblr.com (accessed August 18, 2011).

"Twitter," http://twitter.com/ (accessed July 20, 2011).

Wagner, T. "Rigor Redefined." *Educational Leadership.* October, 2008; Vol. 66, No. 2, 2008.

"Wikispaces." http://www.wikispaces.com (accessed July 20, 2011).

Wiggins, G. *Educative Assessment: Designing Assessments to Inform and Improve Student Performance.* San Fransisco, CA: Jossey-Bass, 1998.

"Windows Live Movie Maker 2011," http://explore.live.com/windows-live-movie-maker (accessed August 18, 2011).

"WordPress," http://wordpress.org (accessed August 18, 2011).